Y0-BNE-042

"... an encouraging companion for traveling the oftentimes lonely path of healing and personal growth. Steve has given me the gift of his warmth and compassion as he shares the secrets to a life of empowerment."

Dr. Cassandra Diamond-Friedman, Ph.D., Author of *Alcoholism in The Gay and Lesbian Community/A Guide for the Helping Clinician*

"Steve shows us an important direction–road map included–that we need to travel for our personal expansion and mankind's evolution. This awareness will assist us in finding the bridge to a New World–a more conscious existence."

Louise Hauck

"... required reading for anyone wanting to live their lives to the fullest. Dreams really do come true when you know how to make them happen!"

Dr. Mike Davison, Psy.D., Author of *Historical Precursors of Cognitive-Behavioral Theory and Practice*

Moving Mountains

Moving Mountains

Magical Choices For Empowering Your Life's Journey

Dr. Steve Frisch, Psy. D.

ALIVE & WELL PUBLICATIONS
CHICAGO, ILLINOIS

Copyright (1997 Alive And Well Publications.)
Printed and bound in the United States of America. All rights reserved. No part of this book may be reproduced or transmitted in any form or by any means, electronic or mechanical, including photocopying, recording, or by an information storage and retrieval system—except by a reviewer who may quote brief passages in a review to be printed in a magazine or newspaper—without permission in writing from the publisher.

For information, please contact
Alive And Well Publications,
858 W. Armitage, Suite 172,
Chicago, Illinois, 60614,
(773) 477-8959.

First printing 1997.

Although the author and publisher have made every effort to ensure the accuracy and completeness of information contained in this book, we assume no responsibility for errors, inaccuracies, omissions, or any inconsistency herein. Any slights of people, places, or organizations are unintentional.

Book cover and text design by Mary J. Burroughs.

Publisher's Cataloging in Publication

Frisch, Steve.
  Moving mountains : magical choices for empowering your life's journey / Steve Frisch.
  p. cm.
  Preassigned LCCN: 96-84736
  ISBN 0-9651511-1-5

1. Self-actualization (Psychology).   I. Title.
BF637.S4F75 1997   158.1
                             QBI96-40205

For years I have been the collector of a wide variety of quotations. Too often, however I carelessly neglected to note sources. In preparing this book I have spent countless hours attempting, unsuccessfully to locate the origins of some of the quotations cited. If you know the sources please contact me at the numbers listed in this book. My apologies to the authors, and to the readers for the absence of credit.

ATTENTION ORGANIZATIONS, CORPORATIONS, HEALING CENTERS, AND SCHOOLS OF SPIRITUAL DEVELOPMENT:

Quantity discounts are available on bulk purchases of this book for educational purposes, fund raising, or gift giving. Special books, booklets, or book excerpts can be created to fit specific needs for promotion of your organizational missions.
For information, please contact
Alive And Well Publications, 858 W. Armitage, Suite 172
Chicago, IL, 60614 or call (773) 477-8959.

Table of Contents

   xx   About the Author

 xxiii About the Pathfinders Programs

   29   There Has To Be A Smarter Way!

   39   What Hinders Our Personal Empowerment?

   47   The Forces of Empowerment Or The Forces of Imprisonment

   57   The Power of Choices

   75   Universal Obstacles To Personal Empowerment

   87   How To Navigate The Universal Obstacles In Your Path

111 How We Approach The Circumstances
     Of Our Life

129 The Prism Through Which You
     View Your World

141 How To Expand The Prism Through Which We
     View The World

153 Tools Of Action

163 Risk Taking

179 Tempus Fugit

Acknowledgments

Any creative endeavor is never the work of just one individual. This book is no exception. I received help and support from people too numerous to mention.

However, I especially want to thank Donna for the time she spent reading and rereading the original manuscript. Your feedback was invaluable!

Equally so, I want to thank Susan for taking time out of her busy life to encourage me and point the way. Your insightfulness guided me into shaping this book into what it is today.

To Christine and Bob, your never ending enthusiasm for this project gave me the encouragement I needed when my energy lagged. Thanks!

To our publication designer and creative director, Mary Burroughs, your magical touch has transformed this book into something more than mere words and ideas.

It is impossible to be a practitioner in the field of psychology without being influenced in both my thinking and development by the many great writers in our field. Their names are too numerous to mention, but suffice it to say, the ideas contained in this book have arisen out of the collective body of literature as it exists today. I have only given them a different form.

Lastly, I want to say a special thanks to the most important teachers I ever have had—all the people I have had the privilege to work with throughout the years. Your belief and trust in me has sustained me throughout all the highs and lows of our time together. I only hope that I was able to give you half as much as what you all have given to me. May your lives continue to be all that you have worked so hard to create for yourselves and more!

Dedication

I dedicate this book to the loving memory of my brother-in-law, P. Phillips. You never got the credit, but you taught me what it meant to be a loving son to your parents and the world's best dad to your children.

About the Author

Dr. Frisch is a clinical psychologist in private practice in Chicago, Illinois. He is a graduate of the Adler School of Professional Psychology where he received his doctorate in clinical psychology. He received his Masters Degree from the National College of Education where he specialized in addictions counseling. His undergraduate degree was awarded to him by the University of Cincinnati, where he graduated with honors.

Dr. Frisch received post-doctoral training in two specialties at the Adler School of Professional Psychology. He completed a certificate training program in clinical hypnosis at the Center For The Advanced Study Of Clinical Hypnosis. He also completed a certificate training program in Marriage and Family Counseling. He is licensed by the state of Illinois as a clinical psychologist. He is certified in Illinois by IAODAPCA as a certified drug and alcohol counselor.

Dr. Frisch's first book, *The Comparative Effectiveness of Group Therapy Versus Individual Therapy As Measured By Self-Concept, Interpersonal Orientation, and Degree of Emotional Adjustment* was an empirical investigation of the treatment modalities he utilizes in his private practice. This book was based on a study he conducted to demonstrate the effectiveness of his treatment protocols.

His treatment philosophy has grown out of his diverse clinical background in which he has worked with a variety of different clinical populations. From these diverse experiences, Dr. Frisch has assimilated a variety of assessment and treatment interventions into his integrated treatment philosophy.

Dr. Frisch has worked on the staff of both inpatient and outpatient chemical dependency programs. This experience provided the foundation for his work with the issues that arise from the impact of chemical dependency on the individual, the family, and the workplace.

As a result of his work in the field of chemical dependency, Dr. Frisch founded the Adult Children Institute. This treatment clinic specialized in working with adults who were raised in families that were emotionally organized around the influences of drugs and alcohol, sexual and physical abuse, and emotional neglect.

The Adult Children Institute developed treatment interventions that enabled the program's participants to develop effective ways to heal from the aftereffects of the trauma they experienced from their earlier development. These aftereffects included substance abuse, depression, anxiety, low self-esteem, shame, and relationship issues such as fear of emotional intimacy and commitment.

Dr. Frisch co-developed and was the coordinator of a mental health program for homeless adults who required treatment for substance abuse and emotional disorders. He developed an individualized assessment and treatment protocol that provided the impetus and support for each individual to rebuild their lives within their local communities.

The Pathfinders programs represent the integration of Dr. Frisch's ongoing research and work in the area of human growth and potential development. Program participants develop the necessary awareness and skills to create an empowered life that maximizes their full potential for both their interpersonal and professional lives.

Whether by individual consultation, group experiences, workshops, or seminars, Dr. Frisch engages his audiences with a mixture of common sense and sound psychological principles of change that awakens and inspires his audiences to the possibility of what their lives can potentially become. He consults with individuals, couples, groups, and organizations that are seeking to implement the principles of development, change, and growth in their lives.

About the *Pathfinders Programs*

"It has been said that a miracle is the result of causes with which we are unacquainted. Once these causes are discovered, we no longer have a miracle, but natural law." This quote, by Robert Parish, has served as a guiding light for both my personal and professional growth. And it has been my privilege to share a very personal journey with people just like you who have discovered their own natural laws from which their own miracles have occurred.

The Pathfinders personal growth programs were born from the very simple proposition that our life's journey is a miracle waiting to unfold. We merely need to discover our own natural laws as we develop the skills necessary to set us free. For our emotional and spiritual well-being evolves from our willingness to combine the truth of our own natural laws with the skills necessary to activate the seeds of the unused potential that lives within each and everyone of us.

There are but two premises you need embrace as you search for your own path on your life's journey. The first premise was articulated over two thousand years ago by Aristotle who said, "People are able to change only by *practicing* the right actions." Very simply, habits are powerful forces that cannot be let go of all at once; rather, shifts in our thinking, our behavior, our emotions and our lives happen through practice over time.

Pathfinders is an essential *living laboratory* where people safely practice the *right actions* that will enhance their emotional and spiritual well-being. The principles of the Pathfinders programs serve as a catalyst for growth—growth created by our willingness to choose new ways of solving the problems we are experiencing in our lives.

But more than just a spark for change and growth, the Pathfinders series is a skills-based program. The primary focus of the Pathfinders series is mastering the skills necessary to enhance each participant's emotional well-being by developing better relationships with themselves and the people in their lives.

The second premise is equally important. Our life's journey is a process to be experienced; not a series of problems to be solved. The implications of this premise are profound for how we approach our life's journey as well as how we define ourselves.

Our life's journey is not a process of repairing who we are for we are not broken. Our life's journey is an ongoing process of creating a purpose in our lives through the relationships we establish with ourselves, with the people in our life, and our own personal spiritual power.

Our life's journey is an adventure. We are seeking to discover the essential truths about the essence of who we are. As we piece together the tapestry of who we are, we are more able to live a life that honors who we are.

We cannot define ourselves by the symptoms we are experiencing for we are not the sum total of our life's problems. We are not dysfunctional souls drifting through life in search of the perfect cure that somebody else possesses, for all of our solutions live within ourselves.

You see, our desire for change evolves out of the same longings we all possess. We all are stirred by the same passions. And we begin to search for our path when those strong stirrings from deep within ourselves are awakened.

These stirrings are the rumblings of something that has long been immobile and silent, cramped and almost dead to the touch. But our emerging hopefulness stimulates our life energy to flow in new and different directions.

And when we discover our own natural laws. When we discover the laws by which we can mobilize our inner strengths and courage to experiment with new choices, we will have discovered the power that lives within each and everyone of us. As we discover the means by which we can tap into our own personal power, we will start to see the challenges in our lives very differently.

We will begin to see the obstacles in our path as gifts that can set us free rather than as obstacles that imprison our spirit. Gifts that can teach us about ourselves as well as open our souls to the possibilities of what our lives can become.

As you acquaint yourself with the Pathfinders series, you will see yourself reflected within the pages of this book. The words on each page will take on a very personal meaning to you—a meaning meant to awaken your soul to the possibilities of what your life can be.

As the tiny seeds of hope and potential that lives within you are activated, be ready for what your life will become. For your life will become a wondrous mixture of hope and fear, growth and paralysis, excitement and discouragement.

And that's as it should be. But over time, the roller coaster ride will even out for you, of that you can be sure. And as it does, you will have trouble recognizing who is staring back at you as you look in the mirror everyday.

Let me share this one last thought with you as you begin your journey. We have a saying that describes people's experience in the Pathfinders programs.

"You couldn't pay me a million dollars to do it again, but you couldn't pay me ten million dollars to have never done it at all."

It is with this spirit that I encourage you to launch your own search for the path that will [re]connect you to your life's journey.

There Has To Be A Smarter Way!

But there is another way that the discipline of psychology can be put to use. It is in helping answer the question: Given that we are who we are, with whatever hang-ups and repressions, what can we do to improve our future.

- Mihaly Csikszentmihaly

A traveler once asked a farmer for directions to a nearby town.

The farmer replied, "Well, after you go down the road for three miles, turn right at the fork in the road. No, that won't work.

"Why don't you try turning around and driving for a mile until you get to the gas station, then turn left..." the farmer continued. "No, that won't work either."

The farmer paused, deep in thought and said, "You know what, my friend? You can't get there from here!"

Well, of course we know this isn't true, you can always get to where you're going. You just have to know what principles to follow to get to where you want to be in your life's journey.

As a clinical psychologist, I often work with people who are seeking to get there from here. How about you? From where are you starting and where is it that you want to be?

- Do you feel like a second-class citizen?
- Do you feel as if you have no control over your life at work or at home?
- Do you back down to keep the peace rather than assert yourself?
- Do you feel as if life is a catastrophe always seeking you out?
- Do you feel as if you are more adept at enduring your unhappiness rather than creating your own well-being?
- Do you feel as if you are always at the

mercy of somebody else's good-will in order for you to get your emotional needs met?
- Do you feel at work as if you do your work and the work of your co-workers as well?
- Do you feel as if you are emotionally drowning from all the responsibility you take on in your life?
- Do you turn to substances such as food, drugs, or alcohol to gloss over the pain you are experiencing?
- Do you wish you could regain control of your life from those who seek to run it for you?

We all are searching for ways to get there from here. Our life is a journey of searching, stumbling, becoming stuck, overcoming obstacles, mastering ourselves and our world, and growing beyond our self-imposed limits.

We all seek ways to expand our lives through maintaining our emotional well-being, creating a life rich with purpose, and empowering ourselves to live life on our terms.

We all are seeking to create a life in which we feel autonomous. We long to feel liberated from all the influences that hold us back, as well as create the circumstances that will support our continued development.

We all are seeking to create in our life an atmosphere of control—that we are the captains of our ship. We long to develop a feeling of accomplishment and achievement in our lives.

We all are searching for ways to develop meaningful

relationships with people. We long for relationships in which we feel valued and cared-for.

The universal principles of personal empowerment presented in this book are the embodiment of how you can get there from here!

Personal empowerment is not just a catchy phrase. Personal empowerment is a life force. It is the process through which we can emancipate, elevate, and expand our lives. It is the process of thought and action combined that moves people along in their personal journey. This book identifies specific concrete principles you can apply to any specific life challenge you meet.

But personal empowerment is more than just a life force. It is a state of mind, an attitude toward life. As an attitude, it communicates courage, adaptability, an eagerness and willingness to experiment and grow. This attitude embodies a spirit of purpose, direction, and perseverance.

Personal empowerment is an emotional state. It is a state of well-being and self-confidence that enables you to overcome obstacles and develop a sense of mastery over everyday challenges. We recognize this emotional state when we feel self-reliant, autonomous, and in control of our life. We see it in our life when we experience life as balanced in terms of manageability, control, growth, fulfillment, and challenge.

But it is even more than all of these things. Personal empowerment describes both who you are and what your life is becoming. Personal empowerment connotes confidence, pride, assertiveness, accomplishment, and being at ease with yourself. As a descriptor of your life, it connotes a life balanced with purpose, meaning, accomplishment, and emotional well-being.

So, my question to you is simple. Is your life shaped by your dreams, hopes, wants, and desires? Or is it built on the expectations of others? Do you live your life as a bold adventure or in fear and timidity?

So many people grapple with these questions.

However, I know the principles I present to you in this book will liberate and empower you from whatever trap in which you may currently find yourself ensnared.

Afterall, that's what it's all about. You grow. You continue to grow. And when you feel empowered, the tides move in new directions, you let go easier, you move with the currents, you are no longer paralyzed by so much fear and anxiety. You may still experience the pain of fear and anxiety, but you will no longer be frozen in it, fixed in it, unable to see what's going on around you. By developing personal empowerment your life will change. You will be able to go with the tides instead of drowning in them.

When you start to see yourself putting things in black-and-white terms, when you find yourself suffocating in a situation where you don't see any other options, you will be able to know how to step back and reframe it. This will mean a great deal in the simple day-to-day stuff of life. You will no longer have a bad day before most people even make it to work!

You will no longer have to look at things so stubbornly, so single-mindedly, so one-way. You will know what to do. You will know how to back-off of something, look away, or step back long enough to gain another perspective. As soon as you find one other point of view, it's a lot easier to see a third, and a fourth, and the multitude of perspectives that exist in every moment of every situation.

You know what you want for yourself in your life. You know where you are today in relationship to where you want to be. The thing you are seeking is a bridge between those two points. That bridge is embracing the process that propels you forward on your journey.

My principles for personal empowerment embody the bridge which is the very life force that can get you there from here.

A young woman came to see me for the first time. She walked into the office, looked around and sat down in the black leather chair in the corner. After about two minutes of composing herself, she began to talk.

"I've never been to a clinical psychologist before. But I need to talk to someone.

"Most of what I need to say may not make any sense, but I came to you to make some sense of it all, so here goes," she said.

"Yesterday, I was at work. My friend, Sue, had been unkind to me at lunch. She picked on the color of my blouse and the way my hair looked.

"Then around three o'clock, my supervisor came up to me and told me that we had more work this week than last week. He asked me to work later and come in earlier until Friday.

"He later came back to tell me that no one else could come in and help, so I should plan on coming in on Saturday too. I sat there when he left, put my pen down, and started to cry."

She looked into my eyes with intense determination and said, "It was right then that I realized that I had had enough. Something inside said 'Stop!' I thought of how all my life I have done stuff because other people have asked me to do it. I ate all my food as a kid, because my Mom said to. I wore special clothes because my Daddy liked them. I hung out with friends and acted like they acted.

"And somewhere I got lost. I let my husband have too much control in our marriage. I love my children but sometimes things are out of balance with them."

I was amazed at this woman's presence of mind.

"When I was a little girl, I was scared that if I did not do what other people wanted me to, they would not like me any more. Deep down, I was afraid they would leave and I would be alone."

By this time she was crying and talking at the same time, so her words were more difficult to understand.

"But when this guy at work wanted me to stay late," she said, "and when I thought he asked me because I was the easiest to push around, I realized that if I ever have a chance to change, it's now."

She had found a moment of clarity in a lifetime built around accepting the will of others.

"I have to find out who I am," she said. "And I'm willing to work hard to do it."

I told her I was amazed and proud of what she had done in my office that day. By being pushed into questioning the reasons for the choices she made in her life, she had taken a huge step toward changing the quality of her existence.

For many of us, life has been a constant parade of backing down, and letting fear make decisions for us. In any given situation, we may pick the choice that ensures momentary relief but may promote long-term pain. And in doing so, we compromise part of ourselves.

So often, we have our personal power taken from us or we give it away. We settle for a life where endurance of pain is valued over the joy of personal freedom. Subjugation and obedience replace personal freedom and empowerment.

If you are like the thousands of people I have met throughout the years, you share the same hopes, dreams, and frustrations they possess. And moreover, you possess the same capacity to empower your life by embracing these very simple principles of empowerment, as they have done before you.

What Hinders Our Personal Empowerment?

*Life moves on, whether we act
as cowards or heroes.
Life has no other
discipline to impose,
if we would but realize it,
than to accept life unquestioningly.
Everything we shut our eyes to,
everything we run away from,
everything we deny,
denigrate or despise,
serves to defeat us in the end.
What serves most painful, evil,
can become a source of beauty, joy,
and strength,
if faced with an open mind.
Every moment is a golden one
for him who has the vision
to recognize it as such.*

- Henry Miller

One day in college, I was sitting in the library. It was one of those sleepy, snowy, winter afternoons. The truth is, I didn't want to work that day. It was more fun to look out the window and watch the chunky snowflakes making their way to the ground through the tree branches.

Eventually, I went to the old part of the stacks and looked through the books randomly. I found one and started reading. I can't remember the title, but it was archaic. In spite of the book's age, I was impressed at what it said. I jotted down a few lines that have stuck with me ever since.

- An empowered life evolves from reevaluating and expanding your life
- An empowered life is congruent with who you are and reflects through your life choices the essence of who you are
- An empowered life reflects the core of who you are — rather than a reflection of what others have chosen for you to be
- An empowered life evolves from a mindset of commitment, purpose, and perseverance
- An empowered life is created through a combination of thought and action
- An empowered life is built upon the accumulated impact of manageable risk-taking
- An empowered life is nurtured through support from the significant relationships you have in your life
- An empowered life's ultimate outcome is a life rich with purpose, meaning, and control

I was amazed at this person's ability to express so clearly these simple yet powerful principles.

I realized although the path of growth and empowerment is a unique, individualized journey for each of us, there are universal principles for personal empowerment applicable to all of us.

Self-imposed limitations create much of the frustration we experience in our lives. Our personal fears create smaller and smaller boxes from which we live our lives. These limitations have eroded our base of personal power and freedom.

The honest truth is we have traded away developing our potential for the illusions of safety, security, approval, and love.

The tiny boxes we find ourselves stuck in reinforce all the things we have chosen to believe about ourselves.

- We believe we aren't entitled to a life created by our choices
- We believe our life choices are restricted to what others expect from us
- We believe we are powerless to effect any kind of significant change in our lives
- We believe we are not worthy of being emotionally autonomous
- We believe we do not deserve relationships that honor who we are

The longer we cling to these beliefs, the smaller and smaller the box we live in becomes. The longer we deprive ourselves of our birthright, the more we demonstrate how correct our belief system is.

I have always believed you can have love and security without compromising your life choices. By developing personal empowerment, you do not have to lose everyone in your life. Living a life rich of meaning and purpose does not mean you have to forfeit all of your worldly possessions. You can expand yourself and your life without living in fear that it will all be taken away from you.

What we need is a process to literally reinvent the blueprint from which we live our lives. Understanding the influences that create our self-limiting blue-print is a necessary precursor to personal empowerment.

Once we find a way to understand how to recognize where we are and see the restrictive influences within our life, we can create an expanded blueprint for our lives.

I have a friend who is tremendously successful in business today. I've written about her before. She loves her job. She makes a great salary and she has an active, exciting social life. And she credits the keys to her empowerment to the things we talk about in this book (although she found them on her own through years of effort).

One afternoon I asked her what her life was like before she figured out the secrets of empowerment.

"Well, I thought everything was fine," she said. "I had graduated from a small college where I met my husband Ted. He was a history student and floated from temp job to temp job, never finding what he wanted to do.

"I on the other hand," she continued, "had a secretary position because I could type. Years must have passed, Ted never got a job. He got bitter, I got nowhere at work and our marriage went from awful to worse. One day I realized I was doing everything to make other people happy, yet I was dying on the inside. I struggled to make changes and eventually I discovered the things you talk about in the book. I don't want to sound too over-the-top, Steve, but that was twelve years ago.

"Today my life does not include Ted. I help direct a company thirty times larger than the one I was a secretary for. Some days I am so happy that I literally begin to cry tears of joy as I have my morning coffee. I tell anybody that if I did it, they can empower themselves, too."

Please indulge me one last story. I talked to a friend about writing this book. I shared with him some conceptual problems I was having with the book and he shared with me some important insights about his experiences with these principles.

He said, "Steve, when you first introduced me to these principles of personal empowerment, I had two very distinct and dramatic reactions. My first reaction was, 'Wow! This all makes so much sense.' I felt excited, elated, and hopeful, all at once!"

My friend continued, "Then I felt an incredible sinking feeling as I realized the depth of what needed to take place in order for me to get there from here. A pervasive sense of being overwhelmed quickly dashed my feelings of elation and hope. I thought to myself that this may work for others but it is too much for me to do.

"Steve, it was almost as if you handed me, one piece at a time, three hundred parts to an automobile engine. You explained each part clearly and succinctly to me and then told me to go ahead and put the engine together.

"I didn't think you could get any more outrageous, but my jawed dropped because of what you told me next.

"I will never forget my reaction when you told me that 'The most important thing to do is to just get started. Don't worry about understanding how the parts relate to each other.'

"You said, 'Just as it takes two sticks to rub together in order to start a fire, all you really need to do is just find two principles that seem understandable and manageable to you and start there. The rest will somehow fall into place as you keep adding new experiences to what you started with.'

"I thought that was an awfully cavalier attitude for something so important. But, you know what? That is exactly how it worked for me. I started with a couple of the principles that felt safest and most comfortable, and things just started to pick-up steam from there.

"Honestly, Steve," he said, "I haven't mastered all the different principles, but what a difference the ones I have become comfortable with have already made. There are some principles I don't like or agree with — they're just not all for me. But, that's the beauty of your system. There are so many different ways to get there from here. I was able to do it in a way that was safest and most comfortable for me."

There was one last thing I was wondering about so I asked him, "What does personal empowerment mean to you?"

His forehead wrinkled as he pondered that question for a moment. He then looked at me and said, "You know, that has really changed for me. When you first explained these different principles, I viewed personal empowerment as the miracle I had been searching for. I thought of it as this huge way of being different. I thought of it as something I had to grow into being.

"What I believe it to be now is the cumulative effect of a series of small victories that has added up to an indescribable feeling that is the combination of happiness, fulfillment, disappointment, setbacks, and overcoming any challenge.

"I think of myself differently. I see myself differently. I carry myself differently. People treat me differently.

"These series of small victories have embedded in me the belief that I am equal to any challenge. My spirit is a formidable resource I can use under any circumstance with any person.

"Most importantly, at the deepest gut level, I am able to look fear in the eye and not have to back down from it anymore. I now have an assortment of tools with which to handle any person or circumstance on my journey."

Let me conclude with some advice that has guided me for years and never let me down once as we begin our journey together.

A bit of advice
given to a young Native American
at the time of his initiation:

"As you go the way of life,
you will see a great chasm.

Jump.
It is not as wide as you think"

-Joseph Campbell

The Forces of Empowerment Or The Forces of Imprisonment

*"How does one become a butterfly?" she asked.
"You must want to fly so much that you
are willing to give up being a caterpillar."*

- Trina Paulus

I remember the day she came in to see me. I was doing some psychological evaluation tests on volunteers to get my masters degree and Pistol had agreed to help. Pistol isn't her real name, it's just something I started calling her after we met. She was younger than my other volunteers, maybe 19. And the conversation went something like this.

"Hi," I said.

"Hi."

"Thanks for coming in, I would like to ask you some questions," I said.

"Oh, this is one of those tests isn't it. I can't stay long, and don't analyze me. OK?" she said.

"It's just a few questions," I offered. "Nothing too serious."

"I bet you guys say that to all of us. Well, I'm not falling for it. This sucks. You and all of your tests."

"OK. First question ... do you ..."

"I changed my mind, I don't want to do this. This stinks. I hate when people ask me questions."

"That's all right, we can stop if you want to," I said.

"Yes, I want to stop." She looked down. "This always happens to me. I start doing something I want to do and then I get scared. Then I back out and feel guilty about being there in the first place," she mumbled as she talked. "I think this is connected somehow but I just can't put the pieces together."

"Well I'm only here to ask you questions, but I think you may be right. If you think there is a connection, there probably is one, even if you can't see it."

"I backed out of going to my Grandmother's funeral. I quit a job after only two days. And, I run out on every boyfriend who gets too close. So far I count three guys I've left," she said. "I think these events all have something in common, but I don't know what. It's like I'm pre-programmed to do this stuff, you know what I mean?"

"Yes, I do know, and no, I don't know what makes you do this stuff. I'm just here to ask some questions, remember?"

"Oh, yeah," she said. "Do you think I'm right about this pre-programming thing. I mean I jump ship on situations that get too tight and my dad goes around getting hurt and dumped by every woman he dates. I call that his M.O., you know, that's Latin, for *modus operandi*. It's his pattern. And he keeps repeating it, over and over again."

"I know lots of people who do the same pattern over and over again. You're right about that," I said.

"I thought so. Hey, this psychology stuff is easier than I thought. Go ahead and ask your questions, Steve."

Pistol's plight is one so many of us face. We are aware of the patterns of our life, but we feel powerless to do anything about the grip these patterns hold on our lives. It's almost as if there is some invisible forcefield that is shaping the direction our life takes.

It is my most fervent belief that we all can create a life of personal freedom and empowerment. We can create such a life through understanding what the components of this forcefield are and how to transform the influence of those components from self-limiting to life-expanding.

And that's what we long for in our lives. We all are seeking a life of purpose and meaning. We derive such purpose from the choices we make on a moment-by-moment basis. These micro-choices serve to construct a life of empowerment, purpose and fulfillment, or a life of quiet despair.

In fact, I refer to this invisible forcefield as our personal blueprint. A blueprint from which the patterns of our life unfold. This blueprint is made from the very fabric of who we are. The combined influences of our personal choices, our style of thinking, the types of action we take, and the impact on our emotional well-being from the obstacles on our journey, all mold our personal blueprint.

We can alter our lives by overcoming the obstacles in our path. We overcome the obstacles in our path by creating different choices for ourselves. We can create different choices for ourselves through combining different thinking with different action.

But it's not just any kind of thought or any kind of action we need to combine.

We need to develop a specific mindset and combine it with some specific ways of thinking about the events of our life. This is the formula for creating a new way of thinking.

We need to harness the power of action. Not any kind of action, however. The type of action that enables you to go one step beyond your zone of emotional comfort. We call that risk-taking. This is the formula for a new way of being.

The true beauty of our personal power is in our ability to consciously decide to better understand our personal blueprint. By better understanding our personal blueprint, we can alter it and increase the amount of influence we assert in all areas of our life.

The following story is a good example of how blind loyalty to our personal blueprint constricts our life experiences as we ignore all the choices that are available to us.

My mom has a fish pond outside her house. She stocks this pond with her favorite fish. A couple of years ago I came across some exotic fish I thought would be a great addition for her pond. Boy, was she excited when I showed her the fish I bought for her!

Well, we went outside to transfer them from the tiny bowl I had brought them in to their new home in the fish pond. While we let them go, my mom was bringing me up-to-date on her favorite stories about the other fish that were in the pond as well as stories about her finch bird-feeder.

While she was talking to me, I noticed something strange about the two new fish. They were swimming in one corner of the pond in the same exact pattern as if they were still in the tiny bowl in which I had brought them to their new home.

I thought to myself how odd that was. Here they had been freed to swim in a much larger environment with other fish. Yet, they stuck to their old pattern of swimming, as if they were still in the tiny fish bowl.

I thought about this for a second. It struck me how those two fish were just like you and me and our loyalty to our own personal blueprint. From our own personal blueprint, we develop our own routine, our own comfort zone, our own habits and patterns, and seldom travel beyond them, whether we have the opportunity or not. We often choose to hideout in our own little part of the world, to stay stuck in our habits and routines, though often times it leaves us feeling isolated, unloved, anxious, and depressed.

Personal empowerment is the tonic that will free anyone from the habits and patterns to which we are slaves. These patterns of behavior keep us locked in our self-imposed prisons. We remain mired in a life that takes us further from who we want to be. Our life remains a mere reflection of other people's will rather than our own personal choices.

STOP

What follows is the premise for the program I have created to illuminate the path to personal empowerment for thousands of people just like you. Do not let the size of this tip scare you away from it. Understanding the tip and enacting it in your life will change your life forever.

Pathfinder's Tip:

The formula for Personal Empowerment is: by creating new and different attitudes plus new and different actions, you will create new and different choices empowering you to overcome any obstacle on your life's journey.

Yes, this one is a mouthful. I promise there are no more like this one in the book.

I have a friend who says it much better than I.

"Steve," he would say, "if you choose to always think what you've always thought, and if you choose to always do what you've always done, then you will always get what you've always got."

I hope this formula comes to mean as much to you as it has to me. This formula is a powerful mechanism of growth that will enable you to develop a life that empowers you rather than imprisons you.

Personal Empowerment Exercise

The purpose of this book is to illuminate the path that will *take you from here to there*. To accomplish this goal, it is critical for you to clearly define from where you are starting and to where you want to get.

The following is a very powerful exercise I first discovered in *Human Change Process: The Scientific Foundations of Psychotherapy* by Michael J. Mahoney. This exercise will help to identify a starting point as well as a specific direction for your journey.

I have designed this for you to do only *one* section at a time, per week, over the course of three weeks. If you feel comfortable, I would encourage you to use this exercise once a month thereafter. You will be absolutely amazed at how your responses change.

On separate sheets of paper, complete the following sentence stems. These sentence stems should be answered as to how you were, are, and will be on your life's journey.

Do A through G in Week I:
a) I was ...
b) I was able to ...
c) I liked ...
d) I believed ...
e) I was not ...
f) I was not able to ...
g) I did not believe ...

Try to list *at least* five endings for each sentence stem.

Do H through N in Week II:
h) I am ...
i) I am able to ...
j) I like ...
k) I believe ...
l) I am not ...
m) I am not able to ...
n) I do not believe ...

Try to list *at least* five endings for each sentence stem.

Do O through U in Week III:
o) I will be ...
p) I will be able to ...
q) I will like ...
r) I will believe ...
s) I will not be ...
t) I will not be able to ...
u) I will not believe ...

Try to list *at least* five endings for each sentence stem.

The Power of Choices

*The way you activate the seeds of
your creation is by making
choices about the results you want to create.
When you make a choice,
you mobilize vast human energies
and resources
which otherwise go untapped.
All too often people fail
to focus their choices upon results
and therefore their choices are
ineffective.
If you limit your choices
only to what seems possible or reasonable,
you disconnect yourself from what
you truly want,
and all that is left
is a compromise.*

- Robert Fritz

I know of a man who accepted dinner invitations every time he was asked. If you planned a party and called to invite him, he would immediately say yes.

In spite of his quick words of acceptance, there was a problem. On the day the event was to take place, he would call to back out. Every time. The excuses were wild and extravagant. It was said that most people invited him just to see how creatively he would cancel.

Sadly, he became the butt of many jokes. And yet there must have been amazing forces at work. Behind the scenes, this man's life was wracked and twisted with conflict and ambivalence.

I don't know him personally, but you can bet there is a powerful force moving him to want to be with people so badly he accepts every invitation. And something equally powerful is keeping him away from all of those good times.

I think everybody knows someone who is severely limited by forces inside themselves. It is quite often more obvious in extreme examples like this one than in our own lives. However, with few exceptions, each of us has something that limits us. We choose to act or not act based on things deep inside ourselves, for reasons known only to us.

For example, a woman I know loves the color red. She thinks red expresses something wonderful and bold. However, she refuses to wear red because when she was a little girl her mother told her that red made her look cheap.

I know a man who wants a relationship. He is handsome, smart, and is willing to do almost anything to meet a woman. Anything, that is, except leave his house. Every night he sits in front of the TV hoping to meet the girl of his dreams, wondering where she is.

There are as many illustrations of this kind of behavior as there are people alive today. And all of these specific examples apply to many of us in some way.

The amazing thing is that these kinds of characteristics can manifest themselves in so many ways. We sometimes say people are unique, even eccentric. Often times, we call them characters. The truth is, we often use such words to merely disguise their idiosyncrasies.

For each of us, understanding our own self-imposed limits is necessary before we can clearly see the choices we do have to move beyond those limits. The process begins with looking at ourselves. However, these limits are often so deeply ingrained in our being, it is difficult to see them.

I know a woman who overcame incredible limitations in her life and learned to make new choices every day. She went from being the target of other people's cruel teasing to being the leader of a large company.

If you ask her to tell you about it, she would say, "What I didn't understand for a long time is my life doesn't happen on the big level where corporate decisions are made. My life happens in the tiny realm of my personal choices.

"I don't need to be concerned about what giant business opportunity is waiting for me around the corner. I need to be looking at the small fears and feelings that percolate through my soul every day."

I asked her once how she saw the difference in herself today, and she said, "For a long time, I wasn't sensitive to my inner voice. I didn't listen to the voice inside of me and follow it to where I deserved to go."

She continued, "In our house, feelings were unspoken. So I thought no one in my family had them. My dad loved me, but he thought being successful was like winning a war.

"You know," she clarified, "for him, success or failure was measured by the direct outcome of any one dramatic event in your life. Yet, what I discovered for myself was success was being able to get on top of the many small battles, fought personally inside myself and my attitudes every day.

"I was afraid," she told me, "to make the choices that got the results I wanted. Most of the time, I put my own limits on just what those choices could be. Other people ran my life for me and I never felt in control."

She laughs about it, and says, "I guess taking a long look at myself has worked! I used to clean the offices of a company that I now own!"

A critical aspect of personal empowerment is overcoming our self-imposed limits. By making choices congruent with the little voice inside ourselves, we honor rather than deny the truth of who we are.

I have my own special exercise I use to free myself from self-imposed limits. Every March 21, June 21, September 21, and December 21, I sit down with a notebook and take the following inventory. Its purpose is to clarify for myself whether I am still the creator of my journey or whether I am allowing my life to be shaped by other people and circumstances. I reflect upon the following in my journal:

- How true have I been to my self-created path in the last three months?
- How have I allowed people and outside influences to sway me from my path?
- How is fear infecting my spirit?
- What do I need to learn from the fear as it is appearing in my life today?
- How do I allow the paralysis of fear to limit the choices I have in my life?
- What choices am I surrendering to my inner fears and my outside influences?
- How can I reclaim my personal power by exercising new choices?
- What of my own personal resources are at my disposal which can help liberate me from my fears to continue on my journey?
- How well am I using these resources to create a life of empowerment and well-being?
- How well am I using the support of others to support me in my personal journey?

Do you see how powerful an exercise this can be for you? For me, it provides a compass to gauge whether I am on my path or whether I have strayed. The exercise allows me to identify why I have strayed and what influences have contributed to straying. As well, I can make a plan of action to correct the direction I am taking.

The points I am always trying to clarify through this exercise are:

- Am I the architect of my life?
- How has my life gotten to the point it is today?
- Is my path created by my own carefully crafted decisions that reflect the unique purpose and direction I want my life to take?
- Is my journey being interrupted by random circumstances, other people's expectations, and victimizing people who keep trying to push me down?
- Do I give away my personal power to the rest of the world or use it as a catalyst in the ongoing creation of my life?
- How am I enlisting the support of other like-minded people?

This exercise liberates me from the quicksand of petty and mean-spirited people, my feelings of helplessness and powerlessness, and the often myopic way I view the world. And believe you me, this exercise works everytime.

Try this exercise now and notice the impact this exercise has on you and your life's journey.

I know only too well how it is for those who don't do anything about their paralysis – a paralysis created by not pursuing all the choices they can create for themselves.

A friend of mine experienced the very paralysis I'm talking about. She allowed her anger and bitterness to deter her from courageously persevering on the path she chose for herself.

She's a close friend and she had just finished her masters degree. However, the experience she had with her school left her bitter. She always believed she was mistreated by the administration. She didn't believe the curriculum properly prepared her for her chosen field. She believed all she received from her two years was a worthless piece of paper—when what she wanted was a marketable set of skills.

My friend was angry with the people responsible for the development of her skills. Each month she went without getting the job she wanted, her resentment toward the school and its program became more inflamed.

Finally, after months of listening to these comments, I asked her a question she found puzzling. One day over coffee, she began college-bashing and I stepped in.

The conversation went something like this, "I never got nearly the attention I needed to better develop my counseling skills," she said.

"Hold it," I interrupted and asked, "I understand how you feel, but I have to ask you, when is this going to end?"

"What?"

"This. How much longer are you going to choose to live your life as an accusation? How much longer are you willing to be a monument to the bad treatment you received from your school?"

I continued, "At one point or another in our lives, we have all felt let down by the people and institutions in which we have invested our time, our trust, our money, and ourselves. And some of us, who have those kinds of bad experiences become paralyzed by what I call the *victim's rap*. It is the never-ending reliving of the facts of our betrayal, and it can leave us short on satisfaction and stuck in a timeless rut."

I leaned back, just in case she might take a swing at me, as I said, "The *victim's rap* is like the frail outer shell of an egg. Within this frail shell is a capable survivor who can overcome any obstacle in the survivor's path. Once we are able to shatter the outer shell by letting go of the *rap*, the survivor within all of us can emerge. Once the shell is shattered, we have the chance to emerge healed and whole.

"Until we shatter the *victim's rap*, the rap paralyzes us, blinding us to what our choices are. Paralyzed by the *rap*, our lives become a living accusation, a monument to demonstrate to the world the betrayal we have experienced at the hands of whomever."

And, for the first time, I think she began to see what she was doing, how she had forsaken her choices by choosing to live in the *victim's rap*.

We all do it. We all, at some point, surrender our personal power by limiting our choices. We do it in so many different ways. And one way is the *victim's rap*.

Or it may be spending the greater part of our lives pursuing the hopes, dreams, and desires of others. We do it for all the obvious reasons. We desperately want other's approval. We desperately want the security of other people's solutions to our life's challenges.

We may be attempting to avoid a life of isolation and loneliness that seemingly our independence will guarantee us. We desperately want to be loved. We desperately seek to live a life free of criticism.

The choice we seem to always be presented with is the same compromise we make by not rocking the boat, rather than enacting empowering solutions to the obstacles in our path.

I have only three questions to ask of you:

- What are the obstacles in your path?
- What choices do you need to make about those obstacles?
- Are you going to honor yourself by creating those choices?

Pathfinder's Toolbox

For those of us who have been sleepwalking through our lives, the idea that we have choices is like being hit with cold water in our face. When we are stuck in apathy, discouragement, or depression, it can be impossible to see the options available to us.

As a result, we mindlessly walk through our journey. Have you ever had the experience of going from one place to another and then not remembering anything about how you got there? That's the kind of experience I am talking about.

In one way or another, most of us find ourselves in a pattern like this at some point in our lives. Sometimes we get there willingly, sometimes not. Fear and self-doubt trap us and inevitably hold us back. Consequently, we repeat the pattern of sabotaging ourselves repeatedly, until we discover the most amazing secret of all.

We have a choice, and there is a way to stop blindly repeating our patterns of self-sabotage.

Our belief system, as we have originally constructed it, no longer needs to be an inflexible, intractable instrument of sabotage and discontent.

Universal choices pave the bridge to personal empowerment. These choices apply to each one of us. The same cycle of choices repeatedly presents itself every time we confront a situation that challenges us to react in new and different ways rather than our old familiar habits.

Universal Choice #1:

We all have a choice between new ways of thinking and our old ways of thinking. How you think about a situation will determine whether you limit your choices or expand your choices.

This may sound simplistic, but there is a single decision we all have to make. A single decision that begins our journey.

Imagine your life as a kingdom, a country filled with cities and hillsides. This kingdom is as complex and intricate as you are. Some areas are prosperous, some stricken with poverty. Some places have many sick people, others are filled with fit, well-toned folks. And just like other kingdoms, your land has room for victims of oppression as well as people who are free. Imagine them all right now so that you can make the single decision that starts to change your life.

With the image firmly planted in your mind, decide where in this land you want to be. Do you want to be a victim or a survivor? Do you want to live in the land of substance abuse or in the land of recovery? Do you want to be in the land of the pretenders or the land of the achievers? Do you want to be in the land of the cowered or the land of the empowered?

It is that simple. You need to make a choice. Go ahead and take a few minutes and think about your choice now.

Universal Choice #2:

We all have a choice between action and paralysis. Life comes at us whether we believe we are ready for it or not.

The second choice is whether to start or not on the path of personal empowerment. I have found that we do not have the luxury of putting off our journey until we believe we are ready.

When you think about it, we consistently deal with life as life presents itself to us. Some of us do it well, and some of us don't.

I have watched many people deal with life over the years. It's my business.

I've found two big groups form when we talk about dealing with life. The smaller group accepts the fact they cannot control many of the things that happen. They roll with the punches life brings.

The larger group seems somewhat overwhelmed with life's adversities. This group has the same attitude as the little man at the circus who follows the elephants around the center ring with a shovel. The question for them is not, "Will the elephant make a mess?" Rather it is, "How big will the next mess be?"

Have you ever heard someone say they will start dating again as soon as they lose 25 pounds? Have you ever heard someone say they will think about starting a business after the economy gets better? Have you ever heard someone say they will ask for that raise after they prove themselves worthy of the raise?

I met a man about three years ago who had overcome a drinking problem. When I asked him what the secret of his success was, he said, "I used to think I was a victim, that my out-of-control life pushed me around.

"One day, while I was trying to stop drinking, I came across a passage written by an alcoholic in *Alcoholics Anonymous*.

It said, "When I am disturbed, it is because I find some person, place, thing, or situation, some fact of my life unacceptable to me, and I can find no serenity until I accept that person, place, thing, or situation as being exactly the way it is supposed to be at this moment. Nothing, absolutely nothing, happens in God's world by mistake.

"Until I could accept my alcoholism, I could not stay sober—unless I accept life completely on life's terms, I cannot be happy. I need to concentrate not so much on what needs to be changed in the world, but on what needs to be changed in me and my attitudes."

Universal Choice #3:

We all have a choice between pursuing someone else's path or being a trailblazer and creating our own path.

The third choice of your journey is choosing a path to follow. In truth, there are an infinite number of paths to follow. The trick is distinguishing between your path and the path others have laid out for you.

How many of you have lived lives of quiet despair because you are in the career your parents picked for you, because you are in the relationship your parents picked for you, because you are in the emotional straight jacket your parents picked for you? Here is a lesson I learned.

One of my good friends is in his late thirties, he's, the vice-president of a bank. Today, he makes no pretense about why he began his career in banking.

He once told me, "When I was little, I wanted my dad to notice me. I wanted to do whatever it took to earn his respect. Well, I was too little to be good at sports. In school, I was good in English but really bad at math. The odd thing is when I got out of college, I went to work for a bank. I worked in the mail room, at first, as a part-time job, but I began to rise fast. Dad was always intrigued by high finance so he took an interest in my career. He said I could finally make something of myself.

"At the time, I told myself I liked banking, but I don't think I did. To give you an example of what kind of skills I had, I helped balance the bank's accounts every night, but my math skills were so poor, I counted on my fingers.

"Even though I work harder at my job than other people, I don't like banking. It took me years to understand I really went into banking to impress my dad."

How many of you are living a life that seems safest to you? The path you're on is safe, predictable, and has already been done by somebody else. How many of you live a life of discomfort because the choices you've made fit you the way a pair of shoes a half-size too small fit you? There is a constant dull ache that never seems to go away.

How many of you live a life of quiet despair because you don't want to risk offending anybody, so you offend your sensibilities? How many of you have bought into the lie that you don't deserve to be yourself, to have the things and people in your life you deserve to have in your life?

The choice of your journey is discovering within yourself what you need to let go of to get to where you want to be. The secret is to find yourself and become that person whom you discover yourself to be.

Personal Empowerment Exercise

This exercise is critical to help you to continually identify the choices you can make about who you are and how you honor who you are.

You will be able to identify how much energy you devote to aspects of yourself that honor you, as well as those aspects of yourself that hold you back.

Being able to choose what you want to hold onto and what you want to let go of will liberate your spirit to honor the essence of who you are.

This exercise will require you to use 10 separate sheets of paper. On each sheet of paper please write the following sentence stem:

"I am ....".

After doing that, read the following scenario and complete the exercise.

Imagine you are all alone stranded in the desert. You have gone weeks without food or water. Your energies are drained as you trudge closer and closer to an oasis.

Imagine 10 separate aspects of your identity, of who you are. Write down one aspect of your identity on each of the ten pieces of blank paper. Imagine how some aspects of your identity are weighing you down in your journey across the desert even more than the rigors of the desert. It is clear that you must shed some aspects of who you are if you are going to make it to the oasis alive.

Now, take those 10 separate sheets of paper and separate them into the following three piles: (1) those aspects of who you are you would let go of first; (2) those aspects of who you are you would hold onto with your dying breath; (3) those aspects of who you are which you cannot decide whether to let go of or hold onto. Be aware of your thoughts and feelings as you do this.

After completing this exercise, take the time to talk over the exercise with an important person in your life. Get their feedback. Use this person as someone who you can practice with as you put into action the choices you have made.

Finally, create a plan where you can routinely do this exercise to sustain the growth you begin to enjoy.

Universal Obstacles To Personal Empowerment

You gain strength, courage, and confidence by every experience in which you really stop to look fear in the face. You are able to say to yourself, "I lived through this horror. I can take the next thing that comes along." You must do the thing you think you cannot do.

- Eleanor Roosevelt

There is a story often told in every bar in Texas about a blacksmith who worked in a small frontier town during the early days of the West. He was known for being the best *smith* for hundreds of miles around. People for fifteen counties relied on him to do the work they needed done.

As the story goes, the anvil he used stood on three thick wooden legs and weighed almost a thousand pounds. Over time, one of the legs became weak with use and one day it broke. The anvil tumbled sideways and crushed the foot of the blacksmith, forever crippling the man.

One day while he was recovering, the *smith* was asked if he was bitter that the career he had chosen had destroyed his foot? To which he replied, "My choices don't bring me problems, my problems bring me new choices."

According to legend, he went on to make the best stage-carriages in the West soon after he recovered.

Think about it, much of living life is really about dealing with the obstacles in our path. By my way of thinking, there really are only two kinds of obstacles. I refer to them as *man-made obstacles* and *universal obstacles*.

How we confront the obstacles in our path influences how effective we are in creating the life we want for ourselves.

For years, I have watched so many people peel back the onion of their lives to discover their individual obstacles to growth. And the voyage for everybody was painful.

I don't think anybody ever said it better than Sylvia, a sixty-five year old bartender who chain-smoked her way through life.

When she laughed, she had a habit of slapping her hand on the table in front of her. Sylvia laughed often. She was a joy to be around.

"Steve, honey," she rasped, "I don't think these poor mopes get it."

"Who doesn't get what?" I asked.

"Everybody, she said. You see, I was watching *All My Children* last week on TV and it occurred to me why most everybody is unhappy all of the time."

"OK. Why?" I said.

"Everybody expects the world to go good for them. And that's just wrong. Life isn't about smooth sailing." She paused to take a drag on her cigarette.

"You see Sweetie, life is supposed to be filled with tough stuff. Most of the people I know who are bent out of shape all of the time are the poor saps that believe that jingle, YOU DESERVE A BREAK TODAY, who said that, Coke? "

"That's McDonalds," I corrected.

"Whatever, Doll. I just want you to get my drift. I think we all have the fantasy that life is supposed to be easy, that there shouldn't be any problems, no struggles. When a problem comes into our life, there are those who feel singled-out, trapped into the delusion they are the only one's who got a problem. All the time asking themselves, 'Why me?' It's sad, really, Steve."

She took another puff, "Everybody ought to realize that we all got problems. Nobody can win thinking they are being picked on.

"Like my Aunt Marge. She went in for a gallbladder operation two weeks ago. She said that God was punishing her for something she had done. I said, 'That's crazy. You just ate too many fatty foods Aunt Marge, no one's punishing you.'"

And you know, Sylvia was right about the punishment.

So many times we believe we are the only ones with adversity in life. We secretly think life should be *smooth sailing*.

It's not nor should it be. It's about dealing with life on life's terms.

Life is really about dealing with the obstacles in our path on our journey.

Pathfinder's Toolbox

Now, as I said earlier, there are two types of obstacles to personal empowerment. They are universal and man-made obstacles. First, let's focus on the universal obstacles. Universal obstacles are experienced by each and every one of us on our journey.

STOP

What I am about to tell you is important. Please take your time as you read along. As you read, think about how this may be true for you.

The benefit of recognizing the presence of any universal obstacles in your life is profound. Recognition is the first step in avoiding your self-sabotage cycles.

You see, our self-sabotage cycles are linked directly to the presence of these universal obstacles. The correlation is a very simple one. The universal obstacles, when present in our lives, create an underlying emotional turmoil.

These obstacles provoke a pervasive fear in all of us. Our fear moves us to implement different means in order for us to cope with our fears.

The rub to all of this is the ways we have managed to cope with our fear. More times than not, our means of coping creates short-term solutions whose long-term consequences are usually harmful to us.

We all wrestle with these obstacles. These obstacles are reflective of the human condition, rather than indicators of our deficiency as human beings.

So you see, the presence of these universal obstacles spawns the creation of our own man-made obstacles. We create man-made obstacles as a means of coping with the fear the universal obstacles stir-up within us.

What I mean is that man-made obstacles are of our own making. These obstacles are a reaction to the presence of a universal obstacle in our path. They exist as a means of coping with our fears activated by the presence of a universal obstacle.

There is an infinite number of man-made obstacles unique

to each of us. But let me make a list, not at all exhaustive, of a few you may recognize in yourself or your friends. After each scenario, I will provide a short explanation showing how the presence of a specific universal fear activates our creation of a man-made obstacle.

Pathfinder's Scenario

When confronted with an opportunity to have an emotionally intimate relationship, we may sabotage the relationship by starting an argument, going out and getting drunk, or having an affair.

Fear of losing ourselves in an intimate relationship is a universal obstacle to emotional intimacy. When confronted with emotional intimacy, our fear of losing ourselves may overwhelm us. We may create a man-made obstacle, such as one of the scenarios described above, as a diversion to cover the presence of the universal obstacle, fear of losing ourselves.

Pathfinder's Scenario

We may be provided with an opportunity to better ourselves in our career by going to school, but we never get around to filling out the application.

We may feel safe with the familiar, no matter how much that holds us back. Being a secretary may feel safe because you're familiar with the routine, and because you're more comfortable thinking about yourself as a secretary than getting an MBA and changing your life. The process of considering change may activate your fear of loss of safety, which is a universal obstacle. In coping with this universal obstacle you may create a man-made obstacle such as procrastination, which allows you to avoid the universal fear. You suffer no loss of safety, because you do not change the familiar.

Pathfinder's Scenario

We may be able to receive a promotion at work if we fill out the necessary paperwork for the promotion, but leave the application in our desk for months.

We may believe our place in this world is being a failure, a victim, someone who never measures up, or as someone who needs to be taken care of. For those of us who believe those things, we may view a promotion as a threat to our place in the world as we believe it must be. Loss of our place in this world is a universal obstacle. We may create the man-made obstacle of sabotaging our efforts by not filling out the appropriate paperwork.

Pathfinder's Scenario

We may find ways to undermine our success in our business by repeatedly doing things that undermine us through forgetfulness, procrastination, or not getting along with the necessary people.

This is a scenario where the universal fear of losing our identity may activate man-made scenarios to prevent the circumstances of our lives from changing. If our circumstances change, how we think about ourselves must change as well. So we create man-made obstacles to prevent our needing to change our identity. If we think of ourselves as a struggler, as someone who overcomes, we will always need things in our life to struggle with and overcome.

The importance in making a differentiation between universal and man-made obstacles is profound. Knowledge is power. You will better be able to transform your personal man-made patterns of self-sabotage into personal empowerment by recognizing how these obstacles exist in your life and discovering new choices.

The universal obstacles evolve from the most fundamental fears we all have.

These fears are:
Fear of loss of our identity
Fear of emotional and physical abandonment
Fear of losing our place in the world
Fear of losing our feeling of safety

Fear of losing ourselves in our relationships
Fear of losing our faith that our world is manageable and we are in control

Please read the next paragraph carefully. Don't be afraid to read it several times. It is important that you see the link between the *presence* of these universal obstacles in your life and how you *choose* to create man-made obstacles that undermine your well-being.

By recognizing these fears and the universal obstacles they create, by recognizing how these universal obstacles present themselves in your life, by recognizing how your man-made obstacles are given birth by the presence of the universal obstacles, you will better be able to navigate the universal obstacles.

Once you learn to navigate through universal obstacles, you will stop creating your own man-made obstacles to personal empowerment.

Sylvia, the bartender I talked about earlier in this chapter, once told me a great story. You will remember that she had a habit of smoking while she talked. And she loved to tell stories.

"Sweetie, you gotta know where you're going or I guarantee that you're in trouble, cause if you aim for nothing, then that's what you'll hit.

"For example, I wanted to lose weight one time and I told my ex-husband Burt my secret, but he never did understand. He died right after that. Hit by a truck." Sylvia wandered around the point to her story alot.

"Anyway, where was I? I told Burt that you have to have a plan. And you need to stick to it. Ya know, move forward with it.

"Burt never understood. He thought I meant only a piece of paper with a drawing or words for a plan. But that ain't it. I think big, I mean a plan like a vision, a dream."

As Sylvia looked wistfully at the ceiling and took a puff on the cigarette, she continued, "Jeeez a girl's gotta dream, doesn't she? And my plan is my dream for me. For losing weight, I kind of start my plan by pretending I look like Vanna White, you know the glamorous super-model who buys so many vowel's on Wheel of Fortune, the TV show."

She leaned back and put down her cigarette. "But in reality, I know that I can't look like her, it ain't physically going to happen. But I can look better, so I call my girlfriend May and ask her to go with me to the store. May is a full-figured gal and we headed to the store so we could buy that Lean Cuisine stuff together, in bulk. Sometimes it just takes two to push a shopping cart, Sweetie.

"So anyway," she said, "after that, May and I call each other every day to check on how much of the food we ate. Before you know it, we both lost twelve pounds. It was tough, but I really wanted to lose the weight, my hips are start'n to go.

"That magic formula works for anything. As long as you're willing. Sometimes you gotta let go of what you need to let go of, and you'll hit a home run every time."

Personal Empowerment Exercise

I have always found it helpful to be able to fight the *enemy* I could see. Therefore, it has always been helpful to me to be able to identify, in very specific terms, what universal obstacles I am wrestling with, the way those obstacles appear in my life, and the man-made obstacles that are created as a result of their presence.

Try this exercise as a way of learning more about your fears and the obstacles they spawn.

> Week 1: Make a list of the ways the fundamental fears on pages 82 and 83 appear in your life.
> Week 1: Make a list of the ways these fundamental fears paralyze you in your day-to-day life.
>
> Week 2: Make a list of the man-made obstacles you create as a way of coping with these fears.
> Week 2: Make a list of different choices you can make to rid yourself of your man-made obstacles.
>
> Week 3: Make a plan of the way you will implement your new choices.
> Week 3: Share this plan with a friend who *will only encourage you*. Implement your plan in tiny manageable pieces and let your friend know how you are doing.

How To Navigate The Universal Obstacles In Your Path

Obstacles offer sufficient proof that everything can be taken from a man but one thing: The last of his freedoms—to choose one's attitude in any given set of circumstances, to choose one's own way.

- Viktor Frankl

A woman I saw years ago in a hospital emergency room opened my eyes to the connection between the universal obstacles in our life's journey and personal empowerment.

When I first laid eyes on her she looked terrible. She was a homeless woman who had been in an accident with a car. From what I understood, it was a clash of wills. The car was moving in one direction, she was walking in another—she lost.

We started to talk while she sat on a metal table with wheels on it. She wore a hospital gown.

"Who are you, the shrink?" she asked.

"I guess so, but I'm really here because I'm in school."

"Then let me educate you," she said without pausing. "How old do you think I am?"

"I don't know," I said and guessed young. "Sixty?"

"Thirty-nine."

"You look older than thirty-nine."

"Kid, I been beat up, I been beat down. And I drank so much, I didn't feel any of it. I look like this because I took every drug I could take and found ways to make the pain most people never dreamed of go away. But I don't do that no more. Do you know why?"

"No." I said.

"A dress I found."

"A dress stopped all of that?"

"Yep, I was sick of being torn up on the streets, and I thought it was the answer to all of my problems when I saw it. Hell from that minute, I walked down the street all summer wearing that real pretty sun dress with big flowers on it. The flowers on that dress made me feel pretty. Then one day I found a straw hat with flowers on that too. So I wore that hat.

"But one day the dress got a bad stain on it. Real bad. People said 'Change clothes!' Hell, people tried to gimmee clothes.

"But, I remembered how pretty the flowers had looked before, so I kept wearing the dress. I thought to myself, 'some people wear stains on the outside, some people wear them on the inside. I ain't gonna give up the only thing to make me feel good about myself in ten years because of one lousy stain.'"

"Did it work?" I asked.

"Well, I didn't take it off for a long time. Then one day I took the dress off for about an hour. I won't tell you why. But, what do you know? I didn't feel any different without it. So I stopped wearing that dirty old dress right then and there."

"I don't think I understand..." I said.

"Then listen carefully Mr. Student. It's because I finally realized that any time you look for something outside of yourself to make you happy, it lets you down."

"You got all of that from a sun dress?" I asked.

"Yep."

I left there that day and never saw her again.

But on that day, I became a wiser student from that one encounter. You see, she made me understand the folly of my ways.

As I reflected upon our conversation later in the day, I decided I needed to learn for myself what my new friend had learned from her experience with her sun dress.

I went home that night and pulled out a notebook. I wrote down twelve questions in the notebook. I spent the next two days searching myself for the answer to those questions.

To this day, whenever I feel as if I am wrestling with something in my life, I pull out a notebook, write down those very same questions and start writing—just the way I did for the first time on that memorable day.

1.) What is the sun dress at this point in my life?
2.) What is the power I am giving to the sun dress in my life?
3.) What am I hoping the sun dress will fix in my life?
4.) Why am I turning to the sun dress to fix whatever is challenging me, rather than turning to myself?
5.) What resources do I have inside me that are more effective and more permanent solutions than a sun dress?
6.) Why am I afraid to use my resources rather than cling to a dirty sun dress?
7.) Why am I choosing to stay stuck with this sun dress rather than get on with my journey?
8.) What lesson is the conflict between holding on and letting go trying to teach me?
9.) What does it mean to me to let go of the sun dress?
10.) What am I afraid of losing if I let go of the sun dress?
11.) What do I stand to gain by letting go of the sun dress?
12.) What is my discomfort with feeling sad about losing my sun dress?

I cannot begin to tell you what a difference that exercise has made in my life! And I can't tell you how many notebooks I have filled up over the years trying to answer those same twelve questions anytime I have had to get unstuck in my life.

Pathfinder's Toolbox

I am going to spend some time reviewing with you the universal obstacles and some possible ways to better understand how those obstacles appear in your life. There is no right or wrong way to review this section. But take your time as you do go through this section because there are many buried treasures in here for you to discover about yourself. I highly recommend you take a minimum of eight weeks to work through this part of the chapter.

The only valuable learning that can come from this chapter is through experimenting with these tips in your life. Knowing the information in this chapter is helpful, even necessary, but it is not sufficient to just *know* the material in this chapter. Tackle these tips one at a time. You can continue reading the book without completing this chapter. In fact, continuing to read the book will enhance the experiments you do in this chapter.

Pathfinder's Tip:

We all become paralyzed with fear as we embark on our journey. What we fear the most is loss—loss of love, loss of security, and loss of self.

I refer to this as the Law of Impermanence. We all would like to believe life is about collecting things we can hold onto and possess. Jobs. Marriages. Freedom. Identity. Prestige. Popularity. Friendships. Houses. Youth. Wisdom. Good health. Cars. Careers. You name it. We believe that if we have it in our lives, we must be able to own it, possess it, and control it.

And the simple explanation is, we are frightened to death of experiencing the pain of losing it.

But the reality is that we all really are only renting our way through life. What we have today we must necessarily learn to let go of at some point in our life. Learning to enjoy what we have while we have it, and letting it go when its time is up, is the most incredible way to live your life. It also is the most painful way to live your life.

We kid ourselves into believing we don't have to go through the pain of loss. But loss goes on with or without our permission. We can freeze our lives to minimize how much we stand to lose, but that requires us to live a life of deprivation.

So many of us are afraid to love, are afraid to go after our dreams, are afraid to invest in ourselves for the fear of one day having to say good-bye to it.

It is this fear that lives at the core of who we are that creates the underlying tension in all of our quests. The fear of loss is the yin to the yang of what you want. This fear is the quicksand we all get stuck in on our life's journey.

These fears are the internal earthquakes we all experience as we navigate our lives around the universal obstacles.

Universal Obstacle #1:

Our fear of dreaming and hoping clouds our vision of what our life can be. Without a vision, our journey is as directionless as a ship without a rudder.

Now you may be thinking at this moment, "Steve, you are a master of the obvious!" I understand that sentiment, but let's look a little closer at the subtlety of this obstacle.

It is obvious you can't get anywhere unless you know where you are going. But think about this for a moment. Are you headed toward something or away from something? Is the path you are on at this point in your life taking you to where you want to be, or taking you away from where you don't want to be?

There is a huge difference. The better part of my day

is spent helping people master the difference. So many of the people I meet know the direction they want their life to take—and that's away. Away from the fear, away from the pain, away from the shame and disappointments in their life.

But they seldom have a vision of where they would like to be in their life. They only know where they don't want to be. And the paradox is the more they run from their pain and fears, the further they get from the answers they are seeking.

Pathfinder's Remedy #1:

The empowered person gives birth to their journey by creating a vision for what their life can be.

So what is it for you? Are you running from where you are in your life or are you running to what you want your life to be?

Take time and figure that out. Sit down and create a vision for yourself. Think for a moment about your life right now. Imagine the things you would be most happy reaching. Your goal may be finding a man or woman to be your life partner. It may be doing something that makes you happy. Maybe it's becoming someone you really want to be. Imagine now that you have three magic wishes to use to reach those goals. What would you wish for?

Let's try something. I want you to stop reading for just a minute and think about your own personal goals. Think seriously about your personal goals. What's your first goal? Write it down in the space below and refer to it when you need focus or strength.

Now think about other goals you can imagine. I want you to set your mind free and think for a few more minutes. Write down as many personal goals as you can, if you need to, use more paper and fold it into this book.

Write your other goals here:

MOVING MOUNTAINS

Universal Obstacle #2:

Our fear leads us to look outside of ourselves for solutions that only live within ourselves.

Self-doubt, lack of confidence, fear of failure, confusion, shame. Pick one or pick 'em all. This is the source of the emotional tornado that rocks us when we attempt to bring all we have longed for into our lives.

When confronted with the choice of standing on your own two feet or handing responsibility for your emotional well-being to somebody or something else, what do you choose?

Do you look to yourself or to others for the solutions to your life challenges?

Do you look to yourself or to others for strength, courage, and soothing?

Do you look to yourself for the creativity to formulate your life, or do you give that power to others?

Do the answers to *your* questions come from you or from others?

The obstacle is fear. The obstacle is self-doubt. The obstacle is believing you can effectively live your life grounded in the solutions of others. The obstacle is believing you can turn to drugs, alcohol, shopping, sex, and/or relationships to distract you effectively enough from the fear that is within.

The solution is discovering how to tap the enormous amount of dormant potential that lies within you.

Pathfinder's Remedy #2:

The empowered person looks within themself to discover the path that leads to their own personal journey.

So how about it?

Do you believe something lives inside you that can propel you beyond your own self-imposed limits?

Do you believe you can reclaim the parts of your life you have given away to others, those parts you have given away to your fears, those parts you have given away to frustration and discouragement?

Look back for a moment at one of your original goals you identified above. Take the goal or goals in which you identified the fears you have in pursuing those goals.

List the ways you have given your power away rather than looking to yourself to accomplish what you set out to do.

_____
_____
_____
_____

Now take your time with this one. This is important and I suspect you have been hiding from the answer for a long time. In fact, don't be surprised if you have to come back to this more than once. But believe me, the discovery will be worth the effort.

List the unused resources you possess, that live within you. All you need to do is awaken them and implement them in your plan of action.

_____
_____
_____
_____
_____
_____
_____
_____

Universal Obstacle #3:

Fear of change inhibits our ability to start our journey.

So, once you've chosen a direction for your life, you *Just Do It*. Right?

Well, not by my way of thinking. If you could easily *Just Do It*, no one would have to be encouraged. They would *Just Be Doing It*.

Quick answers and sound-bite slogans sometimes have

a strange effect in undermining our efforts. Making change sound simple can bring on paralysis in someone who is not accustomed to changing. Change is never as simple as *Just Doing It*, it is a conscious decision to take action.

So once we are at the starting blocks, what keeps us from jumping out to a quick start?

Again, it may seem obvious, but I cannot tell you how many people look at me and say, "I am not the least bit afraid."

But it's quite simple. Fear freezes us in our place. And until you acknowledge your fears, you will continually trip over them. You can act as if you're not afraid. But I have never seen anyone successfully ignore their fears and just throw blind caution to the wind.

So, my question to you is, what frightens you whenever you try to do something with your life? More importantly, how do those fears keep your feet nailed to the ground whenever you try to get out of the starting blocks?

One of the ways we get out of the starting blocks is by learning to risk as we reach for what we want and let go of the comfort of things we no longer need.

One of my friends had been on the verge of divorce. And then one night he called me in tears from a pay phone in downtown Chicago. "What's wrong?" I said.

"My marriage has been over for a long time but tonight I decided to leave the house forever. I know I don't want to be married, but leaving my house and leaving the idea of having a wife is so hard," he said.

Fear always slows us down, but it doesn't have to keep us down.

Pathfinder's Remedy #3:

The empowered person embarks on their journey in spite of their fears, instead of waiting for their fears to go away.

Why do today what you can put off until tomorrow? How many of you live by that credo. Are you just a procrastinator or does your fear create obstacles in the guise of procrastination?

You have just written down things you believe are important for you to have in your life. Pick one of those for this next exercise. It doesn't matter which one — whatever you feel most comfortable with. Once you've picked it, write it down on the first line below.

After you have written down one thing, pause for a moment, close your eyes, and think about what I am about to ask you. What are your fears about creating these things in your life?

Now close your eyes and just pay attention to what images and thoughts float to the surface. After a few moments open your eyes and write down your fears.

_____

_____

_____

Now, that wasn't so bad. So let's go to the second part. Take what you just wrote down and think about the following question. How do those fears appear in your life? Forgetfulness? Procrastination? Excessive eating or drinking? Serial short-term relationships? Take some time and see if you can make a connection between the fear and the man-made obstacle.

The last part of this exercise may be the hardest part, but it is also the most productive part. Who can support you as you try to bring the things that you listed above into your life? Support is the most important part of empowerment.

But, don't run off and tell your dreams to just anybody. Make sure it is someone you trust. Make sure it is somebody who believes in you. Make sure it is somebody who is invested in your growth — not threatened by your growth.

Your dreams are your own personal jewels. Share them with somebody who has the capacity to appreciate them and respect them the way you do.

After you have finished with one of your dreams, be sure you go through these steps again with the other goals you have created for yourself as you feel comfortable doing them.

Universal Obstacle #4:

The fear of the unknown chains us to the prison of what is familiar.

The familiar is the most tempting seductress of all time. We seek out its comfort whenever we are hungry, angry, lonely, and tired. We are attracted to the simplicity of simply doing what we have done repeatedly before. We are romanced by the idea that relief lies in routine and habit.

Whenever I ask someone how they understand how their relapse occurred, how they have strayed from whatever path they have chosen for themselves, they respond the same every time: "I don't know, it just seemed the easiest thing to do at the time."

And I say the same thing everytime, "I believe you believe it was easier, but what I believe is it was what was most familiar for you. As much as you are hurting right now, it doesn't appear to have been any easier for you this way."

Pathfinder's Remedy #4:

The empowered person chooses to let go of the familiar for the promise of the unknown.

The beginning of a habit is like spinning a small thread. Everytime we repeat the habit, we strengthen the strand, until it becomes a great cable that supports our burdens. But we can't create new habits until we start to let go of old familiar habits.

What are the familiar things in your life you choose to keep turning to when you are trying to bring growth into your life?

_____
_____
_____
_____
_____
_____
_____
_____
_____

How does the familiar soothe you in the short-term but hold you back in the long-term?

Who is part of your support system? Who can you turn to when you become overwhelmed by the process of growth? Who can you lean on when you choose not to turn to the familiar ways of coping with feeling overwhelmed?

Universal Obstacle #5:

Our fear of experiencing the losses of what we want to leave behind blocks us from becoming what we want to become.

I talked earlier in the chapter about the grip our fear of loss holds on our lives. It creates caution where spontaneity is necessary. It creates jealousy where fellowship is necessary. It creates pettiness where cooperation is necessary.

This is the one obstacle I see so many people trip over time and time again. Although every aspect of empowering your life is fraught with pain and self-doubt, there is no area of personal growth so charged with pain as this obstacle right here. It is so paradoxical because logically we believe we are headed for a more rewarding way of life. And you are. But in order for you to get there, you must shed some old familiar parts of your life.

For any of us to grow, we will have to leave parts of who we are behind. That may include friends, family members, careers, relationships — even the very way we think about ourselves. We will have to leave behind ways we have defined ourselves, as well as the ways we wanted others to think of ourselves.

This is all very threatening for us to go through by ourselves. As we leave behind the familiar, we are confronted with the darkness of the unknown. We are confronted with the terror of being disconnected from our past.

That is why support is an important ingredient for any

plan of action geared toward growth. The losses you will experience are necessary teachers for your future journey, but they are not things you have to endure all alone.

But most of all, loss just causes grief, pain, and suffering. And those experiences are as every bit a part of the human experience as love, joy, and happiness.

You may not like it. However, it is difficult to move on unless you move through the grief you have pushed away your whole life. And you need to accept the grief that goes with the growth you are trying to bring into your life today.

Allowing yourself to experience your losses as they happen allows you to feel like a whole human being. And that's the most wonderful feeling in the world.

Pathfinder's Remedy #5:

The empowered person moves his journey forward by grieving what he has lost in order to keep what he stands to gain

The most effective way to work through the feelings of loss is to find someone who you can safely talk to about your experiences. As well, keep a record of your thoughts and feelings either with a tape recorder and/or a written journal.

Explore the feelings you are experiencing about the losses in your life. Explore how you can obtain comfort and support from your support system. Examine how your life has changed for the better by the passing of the events in your life.

I mentioned a friend of mine who went through a divorce. Weeks after those calls of crisis when he left the house and took those big first steps, my friend and I sat down to talk again.

"How are you doing?" I asked.

"Better," he said. "I started going out and playing ball with the guys on the weekends. And I think I am going to see a clinical psychologist for a while. Also, I can see the day coming when I will meet new people."

He looked up at me and smiled as he said, "Steve, I need to move on and build a life for myself."

My friend did not arrive at the place he was at by wishing it so, or by asking others to make his life better for him. He endured many hardships along the way. He has many more he will encounter as he pushes forward.

But I know with the basic plan I have just laid out for you, you can confront the challenges in your life well-equipped. I hope you find this plan as useful for you as it has been for me and thousands of other people just like you and me.

How We Approach the Circumstances of Our Life

We are so anxious to achieve some particular end that we never pay attention to the psycho-physical means whereby that end is to be gained. So far as we are concerned, any old means is good enough. But the nature of the universe is such that the ends never justify the means. On the contrary, the means always determine the end.

- Aldous Huxley

We have explored the universal obstacles in our lives. We have discovered how these obstacles stimulate our own man-made obstacles. But knowing that they are there and working through their presence are two different things.

In this chapter we will talk about some of the ways you can transform the residue of wrestling with these obstacles into a small garden of hope and personal empowerment. Before we get too far into this chapter, let me make two points.

First, there is a side effect from creating the new path you have chosen. It grows out of the emotional rhythm everyone experiences when starting to transform and empower their life. Nobody but nobody is immune to it. It affects the best and the brightest people I know. If you stick at working with what you are starting in this book, you will experience it as well.

I saw it the other day when I was with a good friend of mine, Stephanie Phillips. She's two-years old and one of my most cherished teachers. I am always learning something new when I am with her.

She was sitting on the floor reaching for a puzzle piece in front of her. The piece was just out of her grasp. She could see what she needed. She could see where it was, but she couldn't reach it at that moment.

My small friend moved a little and sat. She tried to reach further but couldn't get what she wanted. She sat some more. She thought for a while. Then she sat a little longer. Then my little Stephanie slowly took a deep breath and let out a long deep cry of disgust.

Some people call what I'm talking about frustration. Others call it discouragement. You may have another name for the negative feelings that come from not being where you want to be, when you want to be there. But remember, it affects all of us at one time or another, and you must never underestimate the power of this force in your life.

This discouragement is an abiding condition that can seep into the fabric of our existence. It can be the companion of anyone making the pilgrimage from who they were to who they would like to be. And it manifests itself in so many ways that sometimes it is impossible to notice unless you have a guide along the way.

I suspect this emotional undertow is responsible for many things that are hard to explain. It may unconsciously be responsible for those times when a mother shakes her baby in the aisle at the supermarket. It may be the reason some people sit and stare at the ground all day in the park near my house. And in the most extreme cases, I think it may be the reason some people choose to end their lives early.

I know these are extreme examples, but I think it is important to remember just how overwhelming discouragement can be.

The second point I want to make is to guard yourself against another little monster. It is not nearly so dramatic as discouragement, but it's equally important. I'm talking about one of the waste products that develop from any soul under construction. I'm talking about cynicism.

Cynicism is what happens when you abandon creativity and optimism in favor of despair. It can be really funny to listen to the words of someone who is cynical, but the truth is, most of the time cynics are just looking for center stage by trading angry remarks at the expense of others.

Think about the stereotype that artists face. You know, when you get into a discussion of creative artist, someone will say "Well, I've heard all artists who are good suffer for their art."

What that statement reflects is the conflict and pain involved in any true creative process. Despair and cynicism are real, honest problems faced by anyone who tries to do anything new. That includes any creative activity, and transforming your life is the most creative act of all.

Now that we have touched on one side of the coin, what's left?

The flip side to all of that pain and discouragement is hope. But it is a special kind of hope. It is personal, it is constructive, and it is fun. The flip side of this all is inspiration and play.

This hope is the joy expressed in a wild-abandon dance in the middle of a driving rain storm. It is the magic moment when a young girl discovers the surprise of spinning circles in a long summer skirt for the very first time. It is the joy of a son laughing at the face his father makes as he peeks over the cereal box at breakfast. And it should be a bigger part of your life today.

Creative freedom comes from inspiration. Inspiration means giving yourself permission to play. Inspiration means making time for goofing with no apparent reason. It is a process you must be willing to invest in. It is a commitment you must be willing to make.

One of the best ways to start the process is to let go of as many of the cynical fragments as you can and have some fun with this stuff.

I have put together some of my own springboards to play and I will share them with you now. For many of you,

I know this will seem awkward at first. You can trust in the fact that you will get used to it. And it works!

Just for now, I want you to sit back, roll your shoulders in big circles from front to back several times and take five, long deep breaths.

Notice the tension in your shoulders? As you feel your shoulders roll, let the tension go. Take five minutes to allow yourself to relax in that fashion before you go on.

Now let's move on to five unusual exercises to begin to generate the mindset we want.

Pathfinder's Exercise

Amaze Yourself!

Think of the ordinary things you do everyday and then realize how incredible these accomplishments really are.

For example, if you walk, normally you will walk about three miles in an average day. Yes, if you add all those trips to the kitchen, bathroom, and out to the car you really cover about three miles in a day. That means you walk over one thousand miles in an average year. If you have children or an active lifestyle, triple that number!

Start examining other aspects of your life. How much of what you have created in your life do you view as ordinary, routine, even mundane? We all become blinded by our lives, the sense of routine and ordinariness they take on.

We all need to be able to step back and celebrate who we are today and what we are capable of becoming tomorrow. I am always astounded when what I perceive to be the most profound examples of courage and creativity are just shrugged off by the people whose lives embody such a spirit every waking moment of their lives.

This simple act of reflection has always been a great source of renewed energy and pride for me, when I just examine my life — from where it has come and to where it has the potential to go if I would just allow it to happen.

There is so much power in even being open to what your life has been to this point as well as what it can become. Very simply the power lies in one simple revelation. We are in absolute control of our destiny. Life may inflict an inordinate amount of circumstances upon us, but we have the ultimate power as to how we are going to respond. When we seize upon those aspects of our life that we can control, all of sudden the sky is the limit rather than our perceived misfortune becoming the limit.

It's all very simple! Honor yourself. Honor all aspects of your life. There really is nothing ordinary or mundane about who you are.

Your life is an absolute monument to yourself. Make-up your mind as to what you want that monument to be and how you can think about what that monument is. We all need to celebrate who we are before we can embark fully on the journey to discover what we are most capable of becoming.

Pathfinder's Exercise

The next time you're driving your car, sing your favorite song. Really loud!

The point of this is important for you to grasp. Music allows us to transcend ourselves. We cannot experience our personal power without transcending the self-imposed limits we have created for ourselves. The path to personal empowerment is paved with spontaneity and feeling connected to the possibilities of what we can become. The creation and expression of music is the embodiment of that process.

Music allows us to experience the possibilities of what we are capable of becoming. Music is the coordinated instrumentation of the collective creativity that lives within all of us.

By singing at the top of our voice, we are able to experience a sense of freedom and connect to the sense of the possibilities that exist for us, if we choose to capture the spirit that lives in those songs that are nearest and dearest to us. We must continually plug ourselves into those things that are the embodiment of possibilities. Start with music! It can be fun and send you on your way!

Pathfinder's Exercise

Make friends with an old person.

The value of this exercise is greater than the mere act of doing it. It's priceless. Some of my most cherished moments have come while interacting with the elderly.

One of my friends lives next to a government-supported, assisted-living residence for the elderly. One day, he walked in and asked how many volunteers they had. The director of the place looked up and smartly said, "Counting you, there would be one."

Well, my friend started a six month stint that has turned into three years of sheer love and he's still going strong. He's very clear about the impact his three-year love affair has had on his life. "Perspective Steve, it gives me perspective. I spend my whole week wrapped up in myself and the little world I move in. It has meant so much to me to experience the world through the eyes of older and wiser people.

"Beyond that, my new friends have given so much to me. They aren't focused on the dog-eat-dog world that you and I wrestle with every day. They are so much at peace with themselves so they can focus more on giving to others. That alone has enriched my life in ways that many of my other activities never can come close too. Besides Steve, they have great parties."

Pathfinder's Exercise

Affirm yourself and live your affirmations.

Affirmations have been given a bad wrap. People make fun of their simple nature, but remember, if they were not so effective, they would not have become popular.

Take a few minutes, find a spiritually safe place and let down your guard to try these powerful affirmations. Inhale and exhale five long deep breaths and say out loud:

"There are miracles everywhere."

"I deserve the success I want so much."

"I am lovable."

"I let go of negative thoughts and embrace the creative."

"I embrace laughter."

"I give myself permission to try."

"It's O.K. to play."

"I deserve happiness."

Try this exercise every morning. It can really have amazing results. I have seen them. As you get more accustomed to these affirmations, you can add your own special affirmations to the list.

Our discouragement and despair has deep roots. As children, everything we need to survive is given to us, otherwise we die. And as children, our world is fairly small and complete. We have nothing to compare our existence to—no standards to uphold.

As we grow, we see the world around us and we begin to make choices for ourselves. However, for many of us, the fulfillment and happiness most of us took for granted as children gives way imperceptibly to despair.

And the consequences of that kind of despair can be seen if you know what to look for.

Years of choosing incorrectly leads to disillusionment, alienation, depression, and anxiety. Eventually, for most of us, the pain becomes an expected part of our day. After a while, it goes unnoticed and we lose sight of where we first began.

Then, instinctively, we look for something to make the pain go away. Most of the time substance abuse, compulsive behaviors such as eating, drinking, sexing, and shopping are inevitable distractions we turn to in order to fill the holes left by our despair. It never fails, if you find someone who is a big mess, you will also find that they are in deep pain.

But the helplessness and the passivity that grew from those helpless feelings can give way to a life of empowerment and growth. The learned helplessness of our childhood no longer has to permeate our existence as adults.

You can envision a place you want to be. You can start to let go of all the toxic parts of your life. You can leave behind feelings of discouragement and helplessness. You know you can move forward one step at a time to make these things happen, so do every one of them, and DO THEM NOW!

Pathfinder's Toolbox

The remedy to our discouragement and cynicism is our mindset. Our mindset can immunize our spirit from the ravages of discouragement and cynicism. Our mindset is the most potent weapon we have against discouragement. It is our mindset that allows ordinary people to accomplish extraordinary achievements.

Our mindset can enable us to lift a burning car off a trapped child. Our mindset can enable us to run a marathon. Our mindset can enable us to enact countless acts of heroism and compassion, if we know how to use it for that end.

We cannot empower our lives until we change how we think about ourselves and the vastness of our potential.

The truth is, knowing how to *do* something to empower your life is not enough. The fanciest techniques in the world are rendered impotent without a mindset that recognizes the potential of the *possible*.

Remember one thing about the potential of the *possible*. The most important part about what is *possible* is we have to be ready for those times when the universe opens up to us. If we allow our feelings of discouragement to overwhelm us, we have only managed to set ourselves up to not recognize those opportunities that are available to us when the universe provides them for us.

Pathfinder's Tip:

Action without commitment renders your efforts ineffective and impotent.

The point is very simple. Anyone can learn the simple steps to personal empowerment. However, these steps are rendered impotent without the appropriate mindset. So often we all pay lip service to the means of personal empowerment without enacting a change in our spirit.

The result is always the same: you will feel frustrated and say, "This just doesn't work." Or, "This is hopeless." Often your words can become a monument to frustration and an obstacle often encountered in your future journey.

You can easily see how the times you become discouraged and frustrated your mind begins to play tricks on you. Your commitment wanes as your mind convinces you to pursue a different course or minimizes the importance of the path that you are on. As your commitment lessens, so to will the actions you need to take.

So what's the secret to avoiding this dilemma? It is one of the most provocative yet valuable challenges anyone can master who is entrenched in the process of growth.

Here are three tips that will melt the bonds of your discouragement and cynicism. If you can set your mind to these tips, you will find there is no amount of discouragement that can come between you and where you want your life to be.

Pathfinder's Tip:

An empowered mindset transforms "I want to" into "I am willing to".

A clinical psychologist I know taught me that when someone trapped in the cycle of failure, or alcoholism/addiction sits down to talk, they almost always say the same thing. "Doc," they say, "I don't want to drink or use drugs."

What he told me next will stay with me forever. He said, "The best way you can help them at that moment is to clarify one of the most important principles in the world."

"Tell them," he said, "I believe you when you say you *want* to stop, but are you *willing* to stop?"

At first, I didn't get the beauty of what he was saying. He went on to explain, "You have to help people understand the difference between *wantingness* and *willingness*. You may say you want to lose weight. But if you are not willing to do what you need to do to lose weight, is wanting to lose weight going to get you any closer to losing the weight? Are you willing to exercise on a regular basis? Are you willing to improve your eating habits? Are you willing to give-up your double cheeseburgers and tacos for skinless chicken breast or turkey sandwiches?"

Before you move onto the next tip, take some time and think about this for a moment. What are all the things you want for yourself? Go back to school? Learn how to play the guitar? Take up jogging? Learn how to use a computer? Take that painting class you always wanted to take?

___

Now make a list of each thing you want and what you will have to do in order to have it.

___

After you make the second list, check off after each item on the second list what you are willing to do. See what you can learn from this exercise.

Pathfinder's Tip:

An empowered mindset believes "the only way out is through".

A friend in college once looked up at me from across a library table and said, "You know Steve, I can't believe how messed up my life looks sometimes. I was just thinking about the way my girlfriend and I fight so much, and I hate the way I am. I wish I could just wake up tomorrow and be a different person altogether."

He paused and said, "But I don't think that will happen. I think I have to try and wake up tomorrow and act a little differently. Maybe I can try to change one little thing. Then the next day I can change another little thing. If I keep it up, in about a year, I will have changed several hundred little things and I may have a shot at being the person I want to be. I really believe I can't zap myself out of this situation like magic. Sometimes, the only way out of a difficult problem is through it."

My friend realized that day what we all intuitively

understand. This is all a lot of hard work.

As tempting as it would be to ignore it. As tempting as it would be to do it differently. As tempting as it would be to have someone else do it for us.

The truth of the matter is that the only way out of the circumstances is to go through whatever it is we have to go through. It is the only way to create the circumstances we want. It is the only way to create a feeling of personal empowerment in every fiber of our bodies.

Pathfinder's Tip:

An empowered mindset maintains an unabiding belief in yourself and your journey. Your unabiding belief is the antidote to discouragement and cynicism.

Faith is the wings upon which our journey flies. Without faith, without the belief there is a light at the end of the tunnel, without the understanding that you can achieve whatever it is you can conceive, you will experience your efforts undermined by discouragement and cynicism. Faith, belief, and hope are the most powerful agents of change we have at our disposal. I have seen those three agents melt people's shackles, unlock the doors to self-created prisons, and transform despair into a life of plenty for those who would but believe in themselves and the power of their own unique journey.

I hope you are able to tap into your own well of faith, belief, and hope as well.

The Prism Through Which You View Your World

It is a demonstrated fact of life that you and I do not behave in accordance with the reality of what we can do, but in accordance with the reality of what we believe we can do. It stands to reason that if we change the way we believe, we can change the way we act.

- Robert Anthony

It was a story of two women that had an impact on people around the world. One woman refused to accept conventional wisdom as to what was possible. The other woman was able to transcend her personal limitations. By the refusal of her friend to be deterred by what everybody else considered to be the impossible, they each created a miracle.

One woman refused to look at the other woman's limitations through the prism of her times. You see conventional wisdom at that time prescribed institutionalization of the other woman, keeping her cloistered from the rest of the world. Both women had the courage to create their own world and the prism through which they would view it.

Our parents and grandparents all knew her as if she were one of the family. World leaders listened to the lessons she had to teach.

And her life counted!

The story goes something like this. A baby girl was born to a young couple in a midwest farming community. Their pregnancy had been tough and soon after delivery, the girl's mother realized something was wrong. Her baby daughter didn't notice objects in the room around her. She seemed unaware of everything. Later on, the family found out she was unable to see at all. And to make matters worse, she couldn't hear either.

Slowly her mother and father came to the realization their daughter had little hope for a future. Young Helen was about to grow up in a world in which she could not see, hear, talk, or hope to understand.

As Helen grew, she could only experience the world around her through touch, smell, and taste.

Alone, she was frustrated and angry. Trapped in a life

offering no opportunity for connecting to anyone or anything around her. For everyone concerned, things seemed hopeless.

Until a young woman named Ann Sullivan began to teach the young girl. In time, they were successful and Helen learned to speak using Ann as an interpreter. To be fair, the story of their relationship fills volumes, but for our purposes, it's important to note that Helen and Ann began to tell the world of their ability to overcome adversity. They spent a lifetime communicating Helen's special view of a world seen through the eyes of a blind woman.

The world was amazed by all she had overcome. Her thoughts were profound. A person, who by the standards of the time in which she lived should have been severely limited, flourished.

And her legacy has influenced me. In the following quote, Helen Keller has written a prescription for personal empowerment I follow daily.

> *"Character cannot be developed in ease and quiet. Only through experiences of trial and suffering can the soul be strengthened, vision cleared, ambition inspired, and success achieved."*

The message is clear to me. For you and me, it's important to accept adversity as a part of life. Adversity is not something that can be avoided, because it is part of the human condition. Adversity fuels our journey. It provides the lessons so necessary to our growth, development, and empowerment.

A friend discovered once she stopped fighting to

accept adversity as a part of her world, she could more effectively work with it.

It was a warm summer night. I still remember walking down the street with some friends after a group had met. We were talking, but for the most part the street was quiet. As we slowly walked along, a friend of mine said something very moving to me.

We had been talking about some problems she was going through as we made the walk home. The conversation sagged. She eventually became quiet, as she took time to think about the difficulties she faced.

We knew each other well. She had alot to think about. Then, in the midst of the silence, she looked up and said, "You know Steve, it's true what they say — you really can't control the world ... I guess it's how you deal with it that counts."

Everybody but everybody experiences adversity. For some of us, it presents itself in a dramatic manner, like a near death experience. For others, it comes as the loss of an opportunity, a relationship, or a job. And I guarantee for everybody—yes everybody—it manifests itself like a low grade fever as discouragement and fear.

But there is a powerful tonic available for our discouragement and frustration. I use it whenever loss, adversity, discouragement, or fear creeps into my world.

I step back from what is going on in my life. I find a quiet room in the house. I sit down, close my eyes and listen to a cassette tape on which I recorded a passage I wrote just for this purpose. I do it for about twenty minutes. It helps melt away whatever has infected my spirit. The following is the passage I listen to.

As creators of our personal journey, we value the process of the journey as much as the outcome of the journey.

As creators of our personal journey, we value our own self-respect over the opinions of others.

As creators of our personal journey, we value our own unique abilities and attributes rather than try to become a cheap imitation of somebody else.

As creators of our personal journey, we value personal freedom rather than having to bear the yoke of conformity and placating others.

As creators of our personal journey, we value creativity and self-exploration rather than following the formula of somebody else's plans for our life.

As creators of our personal journey, we value ourselves for who we are rather than what others would want us to be.

As creators of our personal journey, we value our success in life based upon the lessons we learn from taking risks, rather than *playing things safe*.

As creators of our personal journey, we value the endless possibilities of what life holds for us rather than being faithful followers of a script others have created for us.

I hope you will try this very simple exercise when the need arises. It has proven to be a powerful elixir for me over the years.

Pathfinder's Toolbox

Adversity can be a self-imposed prison for many of us. The key to unlock our prison and create our personal freedom and personal empowerment is our mind.

You see, our mind imprisons us and our mind can set us free.

For instance, do you believe the following is true for you?

- We can influence anything that happens to us in our world
- We can control how any arbitrary circumstance influences our lives
- We can resist people's attempts at trying to influence the direction of our journey
- We can make any life choice based upon how we choose to understand the circumstances of our life

I absolutely believe in the validity of all of these statements. We can assert an incredible amount of influence over our lives, more easily than you would ever believe. The secret is how we choose to think about ourselves, the people in our life, and the circumstances of our life.

Nobody! Absolutely nobody, can control our attitude toward anything, as long as we do not give them the power to do so. No event in our life can be viewed as catastrophic, unless we give it the power to be so. Let me explain to you what I mean.

Pathfinder's Tip:

All events are neutral. We color all events in our lives with our own unique and personal interpretation of what they mean to us.

I'm going to tell you a big secret. It changed my life. The secret is that every event which takes place in our world is neither positive nor negative, neither good nor bad—all events are neutral.

That may sound a little odd, but I'll show you how the implications of the idea can be important for you.

Think about the phrase *all events are neutral*. Events have absolutely no meaning until we give them meaning with our own unique way of understanding them.

Let me tell you this story told to me by a teacher of mine, to show you what I mean.

Once there was a poor Chinese farmer. He had very poor land to cultivate and only one son to help him and one horse for the plow. One day the horse ran away. All the neighbors came to commiserate with the farmer because of his bad luck. The farmer sat quietly and asked, "How do you know it is bad luck? Maybe it is and maybe it isn't."

The next week the horse came back with ten wild mares. The farmers came again to congratulate him on his good luck. And the farmer sat quietly and asked, "How do you know it is such good luck? Maybe it is and maybe it isn't."

A week later, his only son, riding one of the wild horses, was thrown and broke his leg. Now the farmer had no son to help him. The neighbors came to commiserate and deplore his bad luck. Again, he sat quietly and asked, "How do you know it is bad luck? Maybe it is and maybe it isn't."

The following week, a war broke out and soldiers came through the valley conscripting all the young men except the farmer's only son who did not have to go because of his broken leg.

Now think about this tip for a moment. Consider what importance this tip may hold for you. What value is there in understanding the following? Our attitudes toward ourselves, the people in our lives, and the circumstances of our lives constitute our own unique, subjective version of reality.

The importance very simply is that we hold the ultimate power as to how we create our lives. Can you see how this point demonstrates the fact we assert the ultimate influence over our lives. Not your boss. Not your out-of-control children. Not an uncertain economy. Not an unstable relationship.

Those are merely circumstances. How we view those circumstances through the prism of our mind determines our destiny. It determines whether we live our lives in solemn desperation waiting for a solution to present itself to us. It determines whether we actively seek to shape those circumstances in order to claim the ultimate control of our destiny.

For instance:
- If we choose to think of ourselves as victims, we will see victimizers in every life event
- If we choose to see ourselves as survivors, we will view every perceived obstacle merely as an opportunity that provides us a chance to grow and assert our influence
- If we see ourselves as kindhearted, we will see the world full of people who are deserving of our concern and our respect

Can you see how you have no choice but to see the world through the prism of your thoughts and beliefs about yourself and your environment?

I have a friend who survived a traumatic marriage. Today, though, she sees the world through the prism of a survivor. But back then, while she was in the marriage, things were very different. She explained to herself and to anybody else who would listen, her mistreatment as follows.

She would often say, "It was all my fault—none of it was my husband's responsibility."

The specifics are not important, but, after getting out of the marriage she has become more aware. She is aware of how her viewpoint of herself and how the world treated her kept her stuck in an abusive marriage.

She learned how she brought the prism of her life experiences and beliefs to bear on understanding the events in her marriage.

We were having coffee in a cafe after the divorce. As we sat there, she explained to me how the prism through which she saw the world distorted her understanding of what was happening to her in the marriage.

"When I was in the marriage, when it was happening to me, I believed it was all totally my fault. I honestly felt like I deserved it.

"Steve, my logic told me I must have been doing something wrong. You know, I believed I was a magnet for all the angry people in this world. I just believed they were angry because I wasn't good enough. I believed it was my lot to be pushed down by them.

"Steve, what I believed about myself kept me locked into the marriage. I didn't think I could make it on my own, so I decided to stay there and take it.

"I would think to myself, maybe if I am a better wife, he would treat me better. Maybe if I take care of my appearance more, he would be more attracted to me. What I believed I needed to do was better myself so my husband would be kinder to me."

But she learned. Boy did she ever learn. She learned that the only thing that made it so was her thinking. And as she was able to enlarge the prism through which she viewed the world, she was able to dramatically change her life for the better.

In exactly the same way, I talked to a young friend of mine who had just lost his job. He was stunned and said, "I hate this, they are just pushing me around like everybody else does. I can't figure it out, I must have done something to deserve this. Maybe I pissed off somebody high up in the company without knowing it. I wish things were different."

In both cases, my friends were paralyzed into inaction. They could only explain to themselves what was happening to them based upon what they believed to be true.

Today, I am happy to say, they have learned how to expand the way they think about themselves and the people in their world. They no longer have the same knee jerk reaction to the circumstances of their lives. They have discovered a more flexible way to think about who they are and how they can approach any obstacle they are confronted with in their path.

Right about now you might be thinking to yourself, "That's all well and good for them but what about me? I don't understand what my prism is or how I even wound up with it, let alone what I should do about it."

Believe me when I tell you, you're not alone with those concerns and self-doubts. Let me explain a little more about that ...

How To Expand The Prism Through Which We View The World

Any fact facing us is not as important as our attitude toward it, for that determines our success or failure.

- Norman Vincent Peale

Often I am asked, "How it is that we created our own unique prism through which we view the world?"

Well, we developed this prism as children. We have spent literally a lifetime experiencing events and interpreting them.

If you stop and think about this, how do children learn? They learn in many ways, but one way is through observation. That's right, it's not so much what you tell a child to do as what that child observes others doing.

You see, children are wonderful scientists. They are keen observers of their environment. They are always watching and observing and taking in information. They are always sifting through the data of what they observe and pondering what it all means.

However, as adept as children are at observing things, they invariably are very inept at how they interpret what the data means. Unfortunately, these interpretations, no matter how well-founded or misguided they may be, stick with that child as they grow.

The child eventually turns these early interpretations into law. These laws become the prism through which the child and eventually the adult views life.

The impact of all this is obvious …

- Children who see the world as a frightening place become adults who see the world as a frightening place
- Children who see the world as a safe place become adults who see the world as a playground
- Children who see the world as a place of victimization grow up to see the world as the same

And so it goes. I imagine you could fill up a page of your experiences and the influence they have had on you as an adult. In fact, take a couple of minutes and see if you can continue what I started above as it relates to your own experiences.

For example,

<u>Children who see the world as a place of ... grow up to see the world as ...</u>

_____
_____
_____
_____
_____
_____
_____
_____
_____
_____
_____
_____
_____
_____
_____
_____

The good news is we are capable of changing these laws. And by changing them, we can expand the way we view the world and our place in the world.

That's how we developed our prism. Take some time before you read on. Think about the events of your life. What has shaped who you are and the things you believe about yourself and the world? Think about the influential people in your life and what impact they had on you. Write your thoughts down in the space below.

_____
_____
_____
_____
_____
_____
_____
_____
_____
_____
_____
_____
_____
_____
_____

Now, as to the second part of your concern. What do I do about my prism?

It is very, very simple to do something. However, it is the challenge of a lifetime to maintain what you have done.

I hope you are getting my drift.

Your personal prism isn't something we are going to make go away. It is only something we are going to expand and learn to work with more effectively.

What I am about to suggest to you are very powerful tools, indeed.

All you need for now is the *awareness* that powerful tools exist for you, plus the *willingness* to apply them consistently.

There are two mechanisms we will utilize to expand your prism. The first is *how* you think about the things you believe. The second is *what you do* with *how* you think about the events in your life.

Now, don't get me wrong. Those sentences are simple to write, but incredibly challenging to make happen. I don't say that to discourage you, only to let you know that I understand how overwhelming it must sound to you.

Much of this work is like trying to turn an ocean cruiser around in the middle of the ocean. It can easily be done, but it requires skill, persistence, determination, and courage.

Imagine a world where every event that happened every day had no meaning. It sounds strange, but think about it. For instance, imagine watching an explosion. You would not be able to know if the explosion were caused by natural or man-made causes. You would not know if the blast happened to solve a problem or create one. And most importantly, you would not know how the explosion affected you personally.

Follow me closely as I go through this idea. In any given situation, when we formulate an attitude, we do it by bringing to bear all of our life experiences on a set of facts. We make a judgment on the situation at hand as best we can and then we decide how something does or does not affect us.

What that means is, once we make up our minds to think about something in a certain way, it can be really tough to change the way we see a situation.

The next time you find yourself stuck in a rut of thinking that any particular situation laid out before you is rock solid, remember it is not. As a friend of mine says, "Everything is not etched in stone."

That simple truism is the key to it all. I have always felt that flexibility is the most important coping mechanism we have available to us. But flexibility is more than a coping mechanism, it is an art.

Flexible thinking isn't an exact science, but our ability to be flexible enables us to live in this world in a much more comfortable way. You see, the opposite side of flexibility is rigidity. A rigid life is a sterile life. Oh sure, it keeps us safe. We are never confronted with having to adapt to new ideas and new circumstances. But not being flexible in our beliefs and actions exacts a huge cost on each and every one of us.

The cost? We miss out on so much. We inevitably sabotage our best intentions. We all recognize how it happens over and over again. We all do it. We all have a way of taking an event and putting it into our belief system so that it comes out the same over and over and over again.

What follows are some important steps to transform rigidity into flexibility Remember, you don't have to master these all at once. But the next time you find yourself looking at a problem square in the face, try following one of these tips in order for you to be able to open the doors to the different areas of your life.

Freedom Step 1

All circumstances in your life are a gift. The pain you experience through these circumstances can be your teacher, if you choose to understand what the lesson is.

I have a friend who is a recovering alcoholic. He is a wonderful guy. For years now, he has been sober.

One day we were talking and I asked him how his life improved when he stopped drinking.

"You know Steve," he said, "the year I stopped drinking, I thought everything would get better. But six months sober, my wife left me, my house was taken away, and my daughter was hurt badly in a terrible car accident."

I was shocked.

He continued, "Most people asked me if I was going to start drinking again. I told them, 'No, absolutely not!' I have learned something that has brought a whole new way I think about the things that happen to me. I told them each difficult time was a gift. I could choose to grow from those times and meet my needs sober, or I could drink and run back into a bottle. Then I finally realized, I could have my needs met in a twelve-step group just as easily. And anything I went through drunk years before, I could go through sober now."

When my friend told me this story, I was reminded of the old saying, "Those things which do not destroy you, will serve to make you stronger."

I believed my friend discovered he didn't need to *think about his hard times as hard times.* He chose to see them as a gift. To him, they were the gift of learning how to stay sober under trying circumstances. He could have never learned that lesson without those trying circumstances. And believe me, it was a lesson he sorely needed to learn.

Now think about your life. What are the circumstances you need to start viewing as a gift rather than misfortune? What lesson is the pain you are experiencing in your life trying to teach you? Take a moment and write down three circumstances and the lesson these circumstances are offering to you.

Freedom Step 2

A person is empowered by what he does with what happens to him.

The man I just told you about is in his late sixties. He had a heart attack not too long ago.

When I went to visit him, he said to me, "Steve, I need you to come over tomorrow and take me to the nursing home."

I was shocked. He didn't seem ready for a nursing home.

He went on to explain to me, "You know Steve, I figured if I felt so shaken by a mild heart attack, other people might be shaken as well. So I gave it some thought, and, I've decided tomorrow I will begin to volunteer at a nursing home to help other folks get through their problems."

"Besides," he said, "it will let me focus on somebody else for a change, and get me out of myself."

This is the action component for expanding your prism. Reflect upon how you respond to your circumstances. Do you give-up, give-in, overcome, or do you act at all? What do you like about the action you take? What would you like to improve upon?

Now think for a moment about what is going on in

your life. What action can you take to make those circumstances different. Write down a plan of action in the space below.

_____
_____
_____
_____
_____
_____
_____
_____
_____
_____

Freedom Step 3

Personal empowerment is the process of actively seeking and creating the circumstances that allow you to shape the outcome you want for your life.

Do you react to life or do you make life happen for you? That's all we're really talking about here. Our prism limits the range of choices we see available for taking action. So we often times choose to be shaped by our circumstances.

Are you the kind of person who would lay underneath an apple tree, waiting for an apple to fall into your mouth? Or would you energetically climb the tree and search for the perfect apple to quiet your appetite?

Are you the kind of person who feels defeated by life? Who thinks to themselves, "What's the use?"

When I think about this tip and the whole idea of expanding your prism, I think about the spirit that is required to bring forth the effort necessary to make all of what you desire possible for yourself.

And when I think about that spirit and how special it is, the words first spoken by George Bernard Shaw ring in my ears. I am sure you have heard these words before, but have you ever tried to embrace the spirit of his words in your life?

"Some men see things as they are, and ask, 'Why?' I dream of things that never were and ask, 'Why not?'"

Isn't it time to turn inspiration into action? How can you embrace the spirit of George Bernard Shaw's words as you move forward with your journey?

Tools of Action

Do you know that disease and death must overtake us, no matter what we are doing? What do you wish to be doing when it overtakes you? If you have anything better to be doing when you are so overtaken, get to work on that.

- Epictetus

As you are sitting, visualize the path you want your journey to evolve into. Imagine yourself as you would like to be a year from now. What can you do now?

If you made it this far, you have begun examining the direction your journey is taking. You may not be aware of it, but you have a much clearer understanding of the basic ideas that are critical to enhancing your well-being. I'm talking about your choices, the universal and man-made obstacles, and the discouragement these obstacles can create for you. And the potent antidote to that discouragement: the necessary mindset to create a new way of thinking combined with new action.

In the next two chapters, we will discuss more about the action necessary to fuel your journey.

That's right, the next step is action. Detached reflection won't work here. You need some tools to use in this process of change.

If it's one thing that I have found, when we feel like we have the right tools to climb a mountain, we wind-up feeling a lot more confident about our ability to surmount any challenge we are facing. The confidence we gain when we feel like we have the right tools stems from the fact that we begin to let go of the judgments we hold that we are broken or deficient.

You see, the real truth is that we only need the right tools. By embracing that truism, we can open ourselves to new and exciting adventures. New adventures where we are less concerned about whether or not we are capable of taking on new challenges and more focused on developing the skills necessary to enjoy our new adventures. So here are five quick, small tools, but take your time as you read them, because they are powerful.

Pathfinder's Tool

The Tool Of Balance

Learn to balance your life.

The wisdom handed down from thousands of years ago attributed to the Greeks was "Do everything in moderation that you may enjoy all things."

Any attitude or action taken to an extreme hurts us. This idea is so powerful entire books are written about it, but for our purposes it is important to realize that many areas of our lives can easily become overdone.

A strong feeling about someone can slide into obsession.

A disagreement between two people can become a vendetta.

The pleasure of drinking can become alcohol abuse.

Nervousness about meeting new people can transpose into isolation.

The point here is not to focus on all of the ways our lives reach imbalance. The point is as you discover the secrets to personal empowerment for yourself, this out of balance situation will, without a doubt, rear its head.

Plan time to treat yourself well. Be aware of this pitfall and nurture the parts of your soul that need some help.

Pathfinder's Tool

The Tool Of Acceptance

Learn not to judge others.

Another important point is acceptance. It is an odd fact that every time we set out to work on our imperfections, we find a need to point out every imperfection we find in those around us. You know the old saying, "There is nothing worse than a reformed smoker."

In our attempts to rid ourselves of our perceived shortcomings, we set out to rid the world of its shortcomings as well as our own. My point is that the wound that we are trying to close cannot be wished away within ourselves or criticized away when we see it in others.

Our healing is solely predicated upon the act of acceptance. Nothing more. Nothing less. The key to enhancing our awakening and our own healing is to avoid judging others. That specifically includes small comments made to put other people down. The most common areas we judge others are the areas that hit home, areas such as money, sexuality, and power.

A man recently rejected by a beautiful woman may judge beautiful women. A woman grieving a lost relationship may judge others in a relationship. Individuals struggling with their own sexual identity may criticize homosexuals. The list goes on infinitely.

Pathfinder's Tool

The Tool Of Economy

Work differently—not harder

Often times we can be undone by our own determination. People who are motivated to grow and pursue their life path can often times have their efforts undone by their grit and drive.

The reason is quite simple. So many of us believe the way of self-correction is through working harder at something. How many times have you tangoed with a challenge only to feel as if you are getting nowhere? When my clients are in that position, they look at me with an intense, determined look and say, "I'll work harder at it next time."

I tell them, "Don't work harder at it, work differently at it. If all you do is the same thing you have always been doing, only harder, you will likely get the same result you have always gotten over and over again. Effort is critical, but, if you don't work differently at it, you will only continue spinning in a circle."

Pathfinder's Tool

The Tool Of The Big Picture

Understanding consequences.

A friend once taught me an important lesson. It is a slogan used in Alcoholics Anonymous. The slogan is *think the drink through.*

What she means is, if you visualize the consequences of an action before you do it, you can more effectively choose whether you want to fall into that familiar trap.

Simply stated, we don't have to act on every impulse or feeling we have. We can pull back from our impulsiveness, our desire to flee, our wish for immediate gratification. There are times when our best interest are served by soothing our impulses and feelings immediately, other times we are best served by backing away from some things. The measuring stick—that's simple, *consequences*.

This idea works wonderfully for many similar situations. If you have a problem eating, think the twinkie through. What would the consequences of that act be? If you have a problem with anger, think the blow-up through. What would the consequences of that act be? If you have a problem with any repeated behavior, think it through.

Pathfinder's Tool

The Tool Of Bite Sized Pieces

Break challenges into small pieces.

Anytime we try something new, we feel overwhelmed. You need to keep in mind that no great task is ever done all at once. You must understand the only chance you or I have of ever solving a big problem is to reduce it to many small steps.

Once reduced, you can put your heart, mind, and intellect into your smallest acts. That's the secret to success.

Let's try to put all of these points into perspective.

What makes any solution powerful is that it is created, implemented, and fine tuned by you. These strategies are the ultimate expression of your personal empowerment.

Every action we take, every word we say, every thought we have, begins somewhere. Sometimes we say and do things for others. Sometimes we do them for ourselves. The question to ask right now is, after all, who is running your show for you?

I have asked a number of people that question, and almost all of the time the answer is not as easy as you would think. You see, psychologists agree that the greatest emotional need each of us has is exactly the same. We want to belong. We want to be loved for who we are. We want to be loved by someone who truly knows us and accepts us for who we are.

But sometimes the question of why we do what we do is more complicated than it seems. And we often times compromise ourselves in pursuit of securing a place to belong by conforming to external demands.

I was talking to a large group of people recently and at one point I began to focus on the subject of *authorship* of their lives. One man sat for about half-an-hour and stared blankly into space. I could tell I had lost him by the look on his face. During a break he walked over and said, "I was thinking about what you said and I don't get it. What does the term authorship mean?"

Well it's really simple, authorship means being responsible for your life, like a writer is responsible for a story. You can't control the world around you, but you can control your part of it. Authorship means being the uncontested creator of your life, as far as your potential will allow. Self-creation cannot take place only in your mind. Self-creation requires action.

Risk Taking

Far better it is to dare mighty things, to win glorious triumphs even though checkered by failure, than to rank with those poor spirits who neither enjoy nor suffer much because they live in the gray twilight that knows neither victory not defeat.

- Theodore Roosevelt

I was having dinner one night with a friend. She told me she believes that she understands herself very well but she didn't know how understanding herself would help her solve the huge life challenges she was facing at this time. She asked me the following question.

"Even with everything that I understand about myself, I am no clearer about how to get beyond the second-class citizenship I hold with my family, my inability to decide on whether to get married or not, and my inability to find a career that I like and that likes me in kind. How can I get beyond these feelings of frustration and fear?"

I looked at her for a moment, contemplating the answer to her question. This question certainly was not a new question to me. I am asked this question in one fashion or another everyday by equally sincere, concerned people.

I knew how frightened she was about her future. I knew how unsure she was of her present. And I also knew how terrified she was at the thought of trying to do anything differently.

I formulated an answer in my mind in very precise technical jargon. Then I quickly discarded what I assumed would be a very unhelpful technical explanation of how personal empowerment comes about.

I finally shrugged my shoulders and just said, "You gotta put a little *umph* into your life."

She looked confused and said, "What!!!?"

I repeated, "*Umph*—you know... sort of a magic combination of creative energy and daring—you gotta put some *umph* into your life."

I tried to explain what I meant. There is no way I know of to *comfortably* go beyond who we are today.

We've carefully crafted our lives for many reasons. Some of those reasons are known to us and some reasons are not known. There are all kinds of technical explanations for why that is, but believe me, I don't know any *explanation* that helps a person who is scared and confused take the kind of action needed to move beyond the *stuck point* they are currently in.

That's where my theory about *umph* comes into play. We already know that personal empowerment is the end result of new and different thinking combined with new and different actions. These new and different actions are very specific. We refer to these actions as risk-taking.

You have to take risks. There is no way around it, over it, or under it. You have to be able to step out of your emotional comfort zone to solve whatever life challenges are presenting themselves to you.

I know of no way to transcend a challenge without creating a new way of thinking and acting. Your old ways exist for comfort. They exist to prevent you from feeling anxious, fearful, and overwhelmed for any great length of time. They exist to create a life of psychological comfort.

That is why risk-taking is such an important component of personal empowerment.

Don't get me wrong. I am not suggesting we all turn into daredevils. Quite the contrary. I do not equate risk-taking with hazardous or dangerous behavior. I think of risk-taking only in the sense of taking one step outside of your zone of emotional comfort.

In fact, I encourage you to do so in ways that ensure your emotional, psychological, and physical safety.

A long time ago, I created something called Steve's Private Hall of Fame. It is a book of newspaper clippings, stories, and photos of people, who through the use of manageable risk-taking, expanded their lives beyond the bounds of the limitations imposed by others, their circumstances, or themselves.

One of the people I greatly admire in the book is a man named Bob Weiland. Bob is a marathon runner.

I first became aware of him when he decided to run 2700 miles across America. That is a remarkable feat for anyone to attempt.

Bob is even more remarkable because of the fact that both of Bob's legs were amputated in the Viet Nam war. You see, he propels himself with his arms and hands, while he glides on the ground strapped into a *sled*.

This was a man who was not going to be stopped at what many of us would consider to be significant physical limitations. His life is a monument to the proposition that if you continually take one step outside of your zone of personal comfort, you can get anywhere you want to get in your life despite the circumstances of your life.

Along the way, Bob gave interviews and encouraged people to take risks to overcome their own personal challenges.

I still have the *book* I created from Bob's story and others like him. One of the lessons I learned from making the book is that big successes in life, like running 2700 miles propelled by your hands, is not one giant victory. Instead, it was the accumulation of many small victories.

A friend and I were talking one day. I've written about him before. He sat down and said, "Steve, I think something is really wrong with me and I want to talk to you about it."

He looked down at his coffee and thought for a

moment, "I'm scared most of the time. I never feel like getting out and meeting people. I mean, I feel kind of crippled socially. I stay at home, feel bad, and it just adds to feelings of the loneliness and emptiness I feel already."

I asked him what he was willing to do to stop feeling bad.

"Well, I'm willing to talk about it, I'm doing that now," he said. "And I'm willing to try and change. When I get home at night, I just sit there. I feel so scared to go out. Scared to meet new people. The thought of meeting new people terrifies me. I feel hopeless and alone. It's like I'm sitting in a pool of thick mud and I can't get out."

I told him he was not alone. And we mapped out some concrete things he could do to begin to change.

I explained to my friend what I am about to share with you. It is absolutely foolproof. Don't be deceived by its seeming simplicity. There is nothing you cannot accomplish if you stick to this simple game plan.

You see the key to risk-taking is concreteness. Global plans that contain more of your wishful thinking and less of your commitment to action are doomed before you start.

Whenever I am confronted with embarking on a new project, I map out the concrete steps I will take for the first stage of the new project. *There are two important points in that last sentence.*

Point one, create a concrete plan. Plans must be concrete and specific if they are to be effective. Global goals such as 'I want to be happy' or 'I want joy in my life', or 'I am going to win a marathon race' are great goals. But how are you going to make those happen? What are the specific steps it takes to be happy? In what order should these steps be executed? What resources are you going to need in order to make that happen? Think big but be specific and concrete.

And point two, start with *the first stage of the project.* I never overwhelm myself with viewing how the whole project will be completed. I divide the project into *manageable stages* and then create a concrete plan.

Now the next part of the plan is absolutely critical. Without using this step, you will make things infinitely more difficult for yourself than they need be. After reviewing the plan, I then create a second list of all the things I have to do within this first stage of the plan that are new or seemingly risky. I go over what is risky about each aspect of the plan. And I do something that is absolutely essential for me. *I ask for help.*

That's right, help. I know that my spirit to overcome any obstacle is exponentially increased when I receive support from people who are willing to invest in my well-being.

Now I know, it seems so simple. Just ask for help. Believe me when I tell you, I watch people all the time make their lifes exponentially more difficult than it ever has to be because of their total discomfort with asking for help. Believe me, we can't get to where we want to get in our lives by ourselves. Hold onto this one thought—other people's help is a blessing, not a curse.

As I said, don't be fooled by what may appear to be oversimplified fluff. This formula has moved mountains for me in my life. It can do the same for you, if you just give it a shot.

Pathfinder's Toolbox

For those of us who have been unwilling or unable to take risks, the idea of implementing manageable risk-taking into our life can be awesome. If you are a person who takes risks often, then this is probably old news to you. But if you feel hesitation tugging at your heels every time you are presented with the opportunity to step out of the rut of daily living, then you know all too well what I mean.

In fact, if you are a truly practiced monotonist you fall into the category of what I call the *risk impaired*. That means you probably have been isolated from change so long, you don't even consider options unless you are forced into a crisis situation.

Think about it. Do you walk through your day aware of the choices you have made every step of the way? Or is every trip to the store unexamined and lifeless?

I became aware of the pitfalls of *zombie living* one day in college. I was driving up Lakeshore Drive making my way to school in a small town just north of Chicago. I was working on my masters degree, and it was the last day of finals at the end of a critical semester for me. I had alot on my mind.

As I rounded the bend along the lake, I heard a loud noise and the car started to jerk. I drove into a gas station and was told if I went any further without fixing the problem, the engine would be irreparably damaged.

I had plenty of time before the exams began, so I left the car in the gas station parking lot and did something I had never done before. I got on a bus.

I'm not originally from Chicago. And getting on a bus was something I had avoided for a long time. It made me nervous. Real nervous. I did not know any of the bus routes. So you will understand me when I tell you when I *just got on a bus*, it was a big risk for me. I was thinking about the two final exams for school. I was nervous. So, I got on the first bus I saw. It was just any bus, I had no idea where it was going.

Looking back now, the events of that day seem ridiculous. At the time, I was so flustered about being forced to take a risk, I didn't really think about what was happening. My daily routine was so safe and protected, that once shattered, there were few guidelines to direct my decision making.

Eventually, the bus I had happened aboard found its way to the main terminal and I had an opportunity to get some good directions. I found a new bus and made it to campus in time to take both tests.

But I came away from the whole thing painfully aware of how my self-imposed limitations prevented me from broadening my horizons. The value of stepping out of my zone of comfort provided me with new found confidence to use public transportation to get me places I had been avoiding up to that point in time. My whole world literally opened up for me.

I believe even more importantly, the small victory I had that day gave me the confidence to take other small steps in other areas of my life.

This only served to reinforce the following for me. Personal empowerment is a process. This process is built upon the backs of numerous attempts at taking several manageable risks.

The net effect of these manageable risks was my life has expanded by conquering one-by-one the things that used to limit my life. I have since learned there are three important things all effective risk-takers know.

Do it in small steps. Do it on your own initiative. Do it now.

Pathfinder's Tip:

Big outcomes are the result of small changes.

I had a teacher in school who once noticed how frustrated I was as I was wrestling with an assignment. "Steve," he told me, "doing something—anything so big—is like trying to build a pyramid. Remember, you can only build a pyramid one brick at a time."

To make his point, he went on to share with me something Gandhi once said,

> *It's action, not the fruit of action, that's important. You have to do the right thing. It may not be in your power, may not be in your time, that there'll be any fruit. But that doesn't mean you stop doing the right thing. You may never know what results come from your action. But if you do nothing, there will be no result.*

To this day, those words have guided me whenever discouragement paralyzes my spirit.

Pathfinder's Tip:

An empowered person initiates the steps necessary to get them from here to there, rather than waiting for somebody else to do it for them.

I once had a neighbor who owned a 1927 Model-T Ford. The car sat in his garage. One day I asked him where it came from.

He said, "I used to work in a used car lot when I was young. One day a couple came in to buy a car and this is what they gave for a trade-in. I saw the opportunity and jumped on it. That was forty years ago. It's been here ever since."

When I saw the car, it needed lots of work. The body was caked with mud 50 years old. The engine needed attention. In fact, almost everything on the car was in need of some repair. I asked him if he had ever started the car.

"Not yet," he said, "but someday I'm going to rebuild the whole car."

I asked him if he thought about rebuilding a little bit of the car at a time. And he said, "Oh, I don't want to get into a project—that might lead to a lot of work."

That man died several years ago. At his funeral I remembered a quote from Henry Ford as I wondered about the fate of that old car.

"You can't build a reputation on what you're GOING to do."

Don't you know the car was still sitting in his garage, untouched, until the day he died.

Pathfinder's Tip:

*Tomorrow's opportunities are too late.
Live life in the moment.*

I think almost everyone battles with the idea of risk-taking. When confronted with a challenge that requires taking a risk, tomorrow always looks very attractive to us. I know a man who is an accomplished musician. He is articulate, well spoken, and by the account of most who know him, filled with joy.

One day we were casually talking, when he started telling some stories. He has a way of telling the stories of his life that take your breath away. During a long career, he has performed for many heads of state, international government leaders, even kings and queens.

While he was talking, I matter-of-factly asked, "Looking back, is there anything you would have done differently?"

And he surprised me. He said, "One thing. I would have learned to follow my dreams sooner. And I would have tried to take more risks to reach my dreams."

"But you did follow your dream, didn't you?" I asked.

"I wasted years finding my destiny, Steve. I only regret I didn't take time early on to find where my heart wanted to take me. I'm sure I would have ended up with the same dreams, but I would have had many more years to enjoy it. I think I put things off for far too long."

The ancient Romans had a marvelous way of understanding living. They summed it up in two words. We know they did because these words were inscribed on the walls of public places for everyone to see. The words are *CARPE DIEM* which translates — *Seize the Day!*

Empowerment is not a life of being free from fear, it a life of living with and managing the fear that you have.

Personal Empowerment Exercise

Take time to identify how you have created your life in a way that insulates you from emotional discomfort. See if you can determine how the short-term benefit of such comfort helps you or hurts you in the long run.

Week 1: What is your personal zone of comfort at work?

Week 1: What is your personal zone of comfort in your personal relationships?

Week 2: How does staying inside your zone of comfort help you at work and in your relationships?

Week 2: How does staying inside your zone of comfort not help you at work and in your relationships?

Week 3: Pick three areas in your professional and personal life in which you need to step outside of your zone of comfort.

Week 3: Identify for each of the three areas in your personal and professional life what the next step outside of your next zone of comfort would be.

Week 4: Tell a friend who will only encourage you what your plan is. Be sure to check in with this friend about the progress you are making.

Tempus Fugit

To be what we are, and to become what we are capable of becoming, is the only end.

- Robert Louis Stevenson

Our life's journey is the accumulation of the choices we make while we are alive.

And our emotional well-being is dependent upon how effectively we make use of the time on our journey as we make those choices.

You see, after you eliminate all the obstacles you create to avoid the choices necessary for a life of well-being and empowerment, you are left with but one choice.

We all can choose between following the familiar path, which creates expedient short-term relief but perpetuates long-term pain, or confront our fears associated with the never-before-traveled path of the unknown.

My life in Chicago has provided me with many experiences that have taught me the wisdom of this very simple axiom over and over again. If you have ever been to Chicago, you probably know that it's unique for a big city. I love it because the culture here is so diverse from neighborhood to neighborhood. And because of that diversity, I have had experiences here that I would never have had in most cities.

One such memorable experience occurred on a busy Saturday afternoon. I had gone for a walk and came upon a man preaching in the streets. He stood next to a big chalkboard setup on an easel right in the middle of State Street. He looked pretty strange dressed in an old black coat that came down to his heels, a torn top-hat, and a T-shirt and jeans underneath the coat. I had some time to kill, so I walked over and listened to him preach for a while. At first, all I thought was that it took guts to stand in the street and talk.

But then I heard his story ...

"It's a story about two friends," he said. "Thomas and

Jonathan were their names. Jonathan had gone on for years talking bad all the time. He complained bitterly about how badly the world treated him and how he felt beaten by what he called the *system*. He said he never got the credit for anything he did. Jonathan felt like no one cared about him. In the end, he said, no one would miss him if he went off somewhere and just died. It was awful."

As the street preacher told his story about these two friends, he paced up and down in front of the chalkboard like Groucho Marx as he talked.

"So one time," the street preacher said, "when Thomas had visited his friend Jonathan, Thomas asked Jonathan if he would like to know how to change his world in only five minutes. Jonathan doubted him, but he was miserable and would have tried anything, so he agreed to listen as Thomas explained his plan.

"Imagine someone gave you $1440.00 in cash everyday for the rest of your life. You can use it for whatever you want. You could buy gifts or services or eat well, you would just have to spend the money. I wouldn't tell you how to spend the money.

"But!" Thomas said as he raised his finger, "there is a catch."

"Oh, I thought there would be a catch."

"But it's a strange catch," Thomas said. "If you don't spend it all, the money you don't use would be taken away and you would lose it forever. That's the catch.

"The next day you would have $1440.00 more to spend. The opportunity would never stop. You could spend it as you please. But if you don't spend it that day, you lose it forever."

"Jonathan liked the idea. He talked about all of the things he would do with the money. He talked about the progress he could make with his life."

Jonathan said, "The small things I could get right away. And, once I finish buying all of the material things, I can help others more poor and helpless than I am. I can teach people to read and write once I learn to read and write for myself. I can show everyone how to stop feeling sorry for themselves."

"That's great," Thomas said. "I can see you understand how big the opportunity is. I'll even help you write down all the things you want, so we can keep a list."

"When they were finished with the list, Jonathan sat patiently and listened as Thomas explained the details of his plan for Jonathan to uplift his life."

"The $1440.00 is the 1440 minutes that are in each day. Every day we have 1440 opportunities to try and try and try. Our choice is whether or not we want to waste the precious gift or spend it wisely.

"The truth for you Jonathan is you have an opportunity to do all of those things we have on the list. You can work to buy the material things, or you can spend your time learning to read and write. If you want, you can even spend your time showing other people how to enjoy this gift themselves. But remember, once a day is gone, you can never have those 1440 minutes back again. They'll be gone forever."

By now I was watching this street preacher closely. He was on a roll, and he had us all mesmerized by his story. He asked the crowd, "Do you all want to know the end of that story?"

We all wanted to know.

The preacher said, "Truth is, I am the Jonathan in the story." As the preacher spoke those words, he wrote his name, JONATHAN, on the chalkboard.

"Jonathan is my name and today I can write it for you. And if anybody needs more explaining, I want you all to see that I am spending my time doing what I told my friend Thomas I would do years ago."

The preacher concluded by telling us, "You now have all the knowledge I have. And somewhere in the good book it says, 'with knowledge comes responsibility.' So everybody make your own list, spend your 1440 minutes wisely and get off your asses and do something."

His last line made the whole crowd laugh. Some people even applauded.

I walked away deeply touched by the story of Thomas and Jonathan. I learned from Jonathan that our life's journey is a verb. The quality of our journey is about the action we take.

And the quality of the action we take is related to the personal empowerment we create in our lives. Personal empowerment is the specific manner in which we live our lives. Empowerment is the action we take to enable each of us to grow and create a life rich with purpose. Empowerment is the action we take to transform ourselves from second-class citizenship into our fully-actualized selves.

But let's not kid ourselves. Personal empowerment is a lot of hard work. Creating a life's journey congruent with whom we genuinely are is one of the most difficult things imaginable. It is difficult because we must confront the core of who we are and the fears that permeate the job of living our lives in a manner that honors the essence of who we are.

I can't count the number of times I have sat in a group therapy room or sat across the room from somebody and thought to myself, "This is a lot of work that's happening here!"

And I am only watching the action.

I once had a client look up at me from his chair and say, "I didn't know when I started this that I would have to not only pay for therapy but do all this work as well. It seems kinda lopsided. Can't you just give me the answers or something and let me go home and study for a quiz?"

I laughed at his joke and agreed with him. And then I told him I was merely a guide for his life's journey. My task is to point out the potential of the different paths that lay before him. He must do the work of choosing which path to take, as well as clearing the obstacles from whichever path he chose to follow.

I explained that it was more important he discover his own truths about how to live his life rather than to try to get me to tell him what choices were best for him. If all he did was create his life based upon what I thought was best for him, he would merely be an actor playing a part, rather than a director scripting his own life.

If the efforts at creating a life's journey that honors who you are feels easy and is without the pain of discouragement, you aren't doing something right. This stuff requires effort, your own blood, sweat, and tears.

But, for a variety of reasons, many of us have been fed a message of impotence and hopelessness. We live in a world that reinforces the message of our limitations rather than our possibilities. But for you today, your world can become very different.

For me personally, there was nothing more liberating than the day I discovered who set my limits and who held me down. In my case, the person holding me down was myself.

If you find yourself saying, "Steve, you don't understand, I'm in a relationship where someone is setting my limits." Or, "Steve, I'm in a job where someone is holding me down."

Then listen carefully to what I have to say. Any relationship, any job, any circumstance can be improved if you are willing to work at it by respecting and honoring yourself.

If you are in any situation that is currently overwhelming you, you might be saying to yourself "I can't even imagine what it takes to do that!"

Personal empowerment is a tough thing to embrace all at once. For today, simply realize that it can be done.

For just like the preacher on the street learned, personal empowerment is the accumulation of a series of choices to take small risks that lead you from the path of safety in your familiar ways to the path of fear and discomfort that awaits you on your new life's journey.

All you need to know is you only need to fight the battle fought within the period of 1440 minutes. And anyone can do that.

If you think you need the support of a therapy setting or a support group, trust yourself. You deserve to change the course of your life with whatever means you can find at your disposal.

Even if you don't think you'll need a lot of help, give yourself the opportunity to discover the tools you'll need to activate the unused potential that lives within you.

The results of changing the path of your life's journey are almost unbelievable. It is great to awaken in the morning and feel unchained and free. There is room in your soul to enjoy life once you lift the burdens of self-alienation and self-doubt from your soul.

A woman I know discovered for herself how euphoric life can be. She told me, "All the energy I put into creating the messages of self-denigration and shame are gone. I wake up feeling so light, so fresh, so alive because my head doesn't have to work half as hard on that useless junk."

For you, the journey may be just starting, and it may seem new to you right now. But realize that this is a simple thing to do. However, you won't grow all at once. But you will grow.

Sit down right now and visualize your life and how you can grow into who you truly are. Plan time in each of the next five days to meditate on this simple visualization. And dedicate yourself to the task of growing.

I wish you all the well-being I have found through the various principles I have shared with you in this book. Before we end, let me tell you how proud I am of you. You have read through this book and you have a plan for yourself now. If you can, write and let me know the results. I really want to hear how things are going for you!!!

What the street preacher said is unquestionably true. In reality, there is a responsibility that comes with knowing the answers of life. And in your case, the responsibility is to learn to be true to yourself, honoring who you are on the inside.

I need your help!

I have a request! It is helpful to me when I hear about people's experiences with *Moving Mountains*. If you can find the time, I would deeply appreciate your writing to me and sharing with me how *Moving Mountains* has affected your life. Let me know your success stories. Let me know the lessons you have learned. What has changed since practicing the principles of *Moving Mountains* in your life? I am eager to hear the specifics, but the most important thing you can do is make the connection and let me know how you feel about *Moving Mountains*.

Please write to me at the following address:

ALIVE AND WELL PUBLICATIONS
ATTN: Dr. Steve Frisch
858 W. Armitage, Suite 172
Chicago, Illinois
60614

HOW TO CONTACT DR. FRISCH

Dr. Frisch is a clinical psychologist in private practice in Chicago, Illinois. He consults with both individuals and organizations seeking to maximize their interpersonal and professional potential.

All of Dr. Frisch's programs are designed to enhance each participant's emotional and spiritual well-being. Each program participant is guided on a journey that will enable them to develop the skills necessary to create a meaningful life that expresses who that person genuinely is. This is done by developing the tools necessary to enhance the relationships one has with themselves and the people in their life.

You can contact Dr. Frisch at
Alive And Well Publications
858 W. Armitage, Suite 172
Chicago, Illinois, 60614
(773) 477-8959.

The Secret To Great Relationships?

Searching for ways to make your relationships be all they can be? In *Building Better Bridges-Creating Great Relationships With The People Who Matter Most*, Dr. Frisch, Psy.D. offers powerfully simple skills for enriching your relationships. By mastering and applying these skills, anyone can create great relationships!

But more than a book on creating great relationships, Dr. Frisch opens the door to a new way of thinking about how to enhance your emotional and spiritual well-being through creating great relationships. Discover for yourself the transforming powers of these relationship dynamics:

- **Enrich Your Relationships by Acceptance and Commitment**
- **Strengthen Your Relationship Bridges by Support and Trust**
- **Open Your Relationships by Effective Communication**
- **Create Involvement by Your Offering and Seeking Spirits**

If you are searching for the key to creating great relationships, *Building Better Bridges* is the only choice for you.

To order by phone, call toll free 1 (800) 879-4214

To order by mail, send a check or money order for $12.95 plus $4.95 S&H. Illinois residents include sales tax of $1.13 per book ordered. BookCrafters Order Department, P.O. Box 459, Chelsea, Michigan 48118

12 Exclusive Astrological Diets Personally Designed Just For You

If you've ever lost hope, not weight, the *Sun Sign Diet* will chart your course to permanent weight loss. Developed by nutritionist and medical consultant Dr. Gayle Black, Ph.D., the *Sun Sign Diet* can help you understand the physical and emotional obstacles that keep you from having a heavenly body.

Here at last is a diet that combines the latest principles of nutrition with the age-old science of astrology. Each of the twelve sections of the book includes:

- **A 7-day reducing plan with detailed diet notes**
- **Guidelines on shopping, dining out and entertaining at home**
- **Practical food combinations for each of the twelve signs**
- **Special techniques that allow you to "binge" eat**
- **Lighthearted personalized notes and life-style tips**

Along with it's healthy, natural approach to losing weight, the *Sun Sign Diet* also offers a tantalizing profile of your sexual appetite explaining how this powerful force works with or against your best weight-loss efforts.

To order by phone, call toll free 1-888-SUN-DIET (1-888-786-3438)

To order by mail, send a check or money order for $18.95 plus $4.95 S&H. Illinois residents include sales tax of $1.65 per book ordered. Sun Sign Diet Partners, Attn: Order Department A 530 S. Whittaker St. Suite 372, New Buffalo, Michigan, 49117

A Thinner You Is In The Stars

THE SUN SIGN DIET

12 Exclusive Astrological Diets Personally Designed Just For You

BY DR. GAYLE BLACK, PH.D.